MARCO

PARIS

with Local Tips
*The author's special recommendations are
highlighted in yellow throughout this guide*

There are five symbols to help you find your way around this guide:

Marco Polo's top recommendations

sites with a scenic view

where the local people meet

where young people get together

(A1) *map references*   **(0)** *outside area covered by map*

MARCO ⊕ POLO

Other travel guides and language guides in this series:

Algarve • Amsterdam • Australia • Berlin • Brittany • California
Channel Islands • Costa Brava/Barcelona • Costa del Sol/Granada
Côte d'Azur • Crete • Cuba • Cyprus • Florence • Florida • Gran Canaria
Greek Islands • Ibiza • Ireland • Istanbul • Lanzarote • Mallorca
Malta • New York • New Zealand • Normandy • Prague
Rhodes • Rome • Scotland • South Africa • Tenerife
Turkish Coast • Tuscany • Venice

French • German • Italian • Spanish

*Marco Polo would be very interested to hear your
comments and suggestions. Please write to:*

World Leisure Marketing Ltd
Marco Polo Guides
9 Downing Road, West Meadows
Derby DE21 6HA England

Cover photograph: Place de la Concorde (Kay Degenhardt)
Photographs: Kallabis: (inside front cover, 14, 16, 19, 25, 27, 32, 37, 45, 49, 56, 58, 64, 74,
84, 89); Lade: Elsen (22), Mauritius/Messerschmidt (78), Rossenbach (4), Vidler (46);
Schapowalow: Heaton (30), Nacivet (66)
Extract on p.5 from Paris, by Julian Green, published in bi-lingual French-English edition, by
kind permission of Marion Boyars Publishers, London – New York

2nd revised edition 1998
© Mairs Geographischer Verlag, Ostfildern Germany
Author: Hans Joachim Kruse
Translation: Craig MacInnes
English edition: Cathy Muscat, Emma Kay
Editorial director: Ferdinand Ranft
Design and layout: Thienhaus/Wipperman
Printed in Italy

CONTENTS

Discover Paris

Steeped in history and thriving with energy, Paris lives up to its reputation as the world's most romantic and glamorous city

Paris is the most beautiful city in the world – at least, that's what most Parisians will tell you. Every year, millions of visitors experience its magic and vitality, and for countless people across the globe it is the city of their dreams. In his haunting work, *Paris*, the Franco-American writer Julian Green waxes lyrical about his native city: 'Paris in a thin mist at nightfall, lights reflected in the water, Notre-Dame all white beyond the bridges – no more bewitching landscape could be conceived. We know, of course, that Paris is beautiful, but painters tell us so over and over again with all the authority of their genius, and we find ourselves struck dumb by a city that Manet, Degas, Monet and so many others place before us, so different from what we see and yet so real. What can one say, faced with the Tuileries Gardens under Pissarro's April sky, or the Seine embankment in

The Gothic cathedral of Notre-Dame on the Ile de la Cité in the heart of Paris has inspired many an artist over the centuries

winter beneath Gauguin's snow-laden sky or in Lebourg's roseate dusk? Lips are silent; only eyes have the power of speech.'

Paris can be an overwhelming city at first. When planning your itinerary bear in mind that even if you were to spend a lifetime here, it would be virtually impossible to explore every nook and cranny. So don't put too much pressure on yourself to take it all in during one visit. Naturally enough, most first-time visitors are eager to visit all of the best-known sights. The Eiffel Tower and Notre-Dame, the Louvre and the Pompidou Centre, the Arc de Triomphe and the Champs-Elysées, may be at the top of every sightseeing list, but some of the most memorable sights lie off the well-worn tourist track. While the public transport network is excellent, this is the perfect city to explore on foot. You need time, patience, a good pair of walking shoes and a bit of luck to discover the city's many secluded areas and hidden treasures.

With over 10 million inhabitants, Greater Paris is one of the most densely populated urban areas in the world. As Paul Valéry once wrote, 'Paris is the political, literary, scientific and financial focus of a great country. This lends it a unique character when compared with other large cities.' The poet's claims are still justified and his list of distinguishing features could be easily expanded upon. Today Paris is one of the most important centres for tourism in the world, welcoming over 21 million visitors each year, 11 million of them from abroad. It has more accommodation facilities and catering establishments per capita than any other city in the world. There are more than 13 universities, over 300 cinema screens and more than 100 museums and 100 theatres.

For many years now, Paris has also enjoyed top billing as a conference centre, outshining all its principal rivals – London, New York, Brussels, etc. – which are finding it more and more difficult to compete in this area. But what is it that makes this city so popular? The answer undoubtedly lies in the cocktail of attractions which, when mixed, make it an irresistible place. Apart from its sheer physical beauty, which has been eloquently described by countless writers, the choice of restaurants and bistros, cultural events, shops and boutiques, and entertainment venues is unparalleled. With so much on offer, any trip to the city of light is guaranteed to be a unique and stimulating experience.

Street life is as busy, colourful, and exuberant as ever. The crush of people and traffic can be quite overwhelming at times. Some find the hectic nature of Parisian life all too much; others thrive on

it. On the whole, the western side of the city is still the more exclusive area, while the eastern side remains more resolutely working class. Although it is true that the professional classes are making inroads into former working-class districts, and areas like Ménilmontant and Belleville are slowly being gentrified, the differences are still very marked. That said, the 'more refined' western districts are considered dull by many when compared to the livelier eastern areas.

For centuries, Paris was generally held to be one of the most important – if not *the* most important – cultural centres of the world. During the first half of this century, it became a mecca for artists, writers, and musicians. In the last few decades, however, the city gradually began to lose its cultural supremacy. It was no longer the automatic stage for major cultural events. The art market moved elsewhere as did many influential artists and intellectuals. For some time Parisians lost faith in their city, which was no longer regarded as the centre of high culture. This period of uncertainty, however, appears to be well and truly over. During the celebrations for the 200th anniversary of the French Revolution, the Parisian weekly *Le Nouvel Observateur* claimed: 'Paris is back on top of the world. The city has evolved more in the space of a decade than it did during any of the preceding centuries. The whole world listens to its music, visits its exhibitions, envies its innovation and fills its streets.' As the millennium approaches, confidence is being restored. 'Paris is once more a magical place where talent and energy are synthesized by some mysterious alchemy to produce the essential spirit of the age'. For proof of this cultural renaissance, we need only look at the ever-increasing number of intellectuals and artists who are once again being drawn to live and work in Paris by the exciting and stimulating atmosphere they find here.

Alongside the countless museums, there are over 400 galleries, with new ones opening all the time. The larger exhibitions attract hundreds of thousands of visitors. Art and culture have taken over the streets. Paris is chosen as the location for so many films that it sometimes feels as if the city has been transformed into one enormous film set. There has been an explosion of musical talent in the last few years, with new concert halls, jazz clubs, rock, reggae, African and Caribbean music clubs all thriving quite happily. Developments in architecture and design are astounding. Visit the business district of La Défense, with its futuristic high-rise blocks, the Cité des Sciences at La Villette, or the new National Library, and you get the feeling that we are already in the 21st century.

Paris is becoming an increasingly cosmopolitan city. According to official statistics, over 350 000 immigrants from all over the world live within the narrow city confines. This figure doesn't include illegal residents, tourists, and the 50 000 or so foreign students, not to mention the many thousands of French citizens with either one or two foreign parents. This concoction of nationalities makes the city something of a cultural kaleidoscope, and it is hard to find another European city with such an open-minded and tolerant atmosphere as Paris.

Strictly speaking, there are not many true Parisians left. This is because the official city boundaries are rather narrowly drawn. At its core, Paris only has about two million inhabitants, and even this number is steadily decreasing. This decline in population, however, is not the result of a diminishing appeal. Paris is attracting more businesses, luxury hotels, international institutions, wealthy residents, tourists and conferences than ever before. All of this means, however, that ordinary Parisians are finding it increasingly difficult to afford to stay in a city where the cost of living has rocketed. More and more of them are moving out to the suburbs. This exodus is not just a consequence of the exorbitant property prices. Paris has suffered from an incredible population density since medieval times. With 20 000 inhabitants per square kilometre, it is three times more densely populated than London, and compares unfavourably in this regard to New York, Moscow, and even Tokyo.

Some strange preconceived notions about the Parisian way of life are still held by many outsiders – clichés which are perpetuated by sentimental songs. Listening to these, you would think that the average Parisian is only interested in making love and eating (though not necessarily in that order), and that he is naturally witty, cultured and charming, even when penniless. A similar myth surrounds the Parisian *clochards,* which leads us to believe that the city's down-and-outs are actually philosophers who have found the key to happiness and are leading the only kind of life worth living. These romanticized images of Paris are somewhat dated, and very different from the harsher reality. As in any other major city in this day and age, life here can be hard on the nerves, expensive, exhausting, and sometimes dangerous. Every day millions of commuters have to endure long journeys to work, in intolerably overcrowded conditions, while the roads are choked with traffic, and driving standards are notoriously cavalier. It is fair to say that the average Parisian, perhaps hardened by the chaos that surrounds him, doesn't always overflow with joy and goodwill towards his fellow man.

Parisian *savoir-vivre*, on the other hand, is not just a cliché. Parisians may work hard and get stressed out, but they know how to relax in their leisure time. It's not only the tourists who enjoy lounging in street cafés and on park benches, and meandering along the banks of the Seine. No other city in the world has such a high concentration of restaurants, cafés and bistros. Although it's no longer true that everything comes to a halt for two hours around lunchtime, people who work in Paris still consider eating well and relaxing in comfortable surroundings to be an essential part of their daily routine.

Food is taken very seriously. The knowledge and appreciation of good food and wine seems to be inbred. Try asking a Parisian about the various attributes and qualities of a baguette, watch people at the market sniffing melons and prodding Camembert, or in a restaurant savouring a plate of oysters. But while it's fascinating to sit back and observe this Parisian *savoir-vivre* in action, it's much more fun to experience it for yourself.

'If Paris were not the fashion capital, then fashion would have no capital.' So said managing director of Yves St Laurent, Pierre Bergé. Kenzo, the designer who transformed the Place des Victoires in the middle of Paris into a completely new fashion centre, claimed that 'in Paris, every wall, every passer-by, even the sky helps me to create my collection.' Per Spook, another designer, originally from Norway, puts it this way: 'If you want to be acknowledged as someone who has ideas in the world of fashion, then Paris is the most important place to be – an inexhaustible source of inspiration. This must have something to do with Parisian flair, it's almost contagious. I've tried to design elsewhere, but it didn't work out. For fashion and for myself, it has to be Paris.' Twice a year, in January and in July, the leading lights of fashion from all over the world gather in Paris, when the *haute couture* and *prêt-à-porter* (ready-to-wear) collections are paraded by supermodels on the catwalk. The main events are centred around the Louvre, but the whole city revolves around the fashion industry at these times. Paris is so important for the fashion business that even the largest, longest-established foreign fashion designers usually decide to launch their latest collections here rather than in their own countries.

Strolling through Paris

Monumental Paris (E 3-A1)

The Champs-Elysées is particularly impressive at night. Stroll up from the Place de la Concorde between the trees towards the Arc de Triomphe and the Arche de la Défense.

Chic Shops (E 2-3)

The best place to begin a tour of the exclusive shops is at the magnificent old Opéra building. Walk up Boulevard des Capucines, and then along Boulevard de la Madeleine until you reach the imposing Madeleine church. These streets are lined with wonderful delicatessens and top restaurants. It is not far from the church to the Place Vendôme and Rue de la Paix, where rows of expensive jewellers exhibit exquisite treasures. For the luxurious (and expensive) fashion boutiques, head towards the Elysée Palace along the elegant Rue du Faubourg St-Honoré.

Bastille (I 5-4)

The new Opéra house dominates the Place de la Bastille. Rue de la Roquette is colourful and lively, while the Rue de Lappe and surrounding streets are full of trendy bars and art galleries. Wander down to the market in the Place Aligre, one of the most authentic corners of Paris.

Arcades (F 2-3)

At the beginning of the 19th century, there were over a hundred *passages* – shop-lined thoroughfares protected by glass roofs. Today there are only 20 or so left. Many of these charming arcades can be accessed from the Rue St-Denis. The Jouffroy arcade and the Passage des Panoramas at the Boulevard Montmartre are also very attractive. Go through the Passage Choiseul to the Colbert and Vivienne galleries in the Place des Victoires with its fashion boutiques and on to the Arcades des Palais Royal.

The Marais (G 4-H 4)

Make your way from Notre-Dame across the river to the square in front of the town hall (Hôtel de Ville), and into the old streets of the Marais. On the way to the Place des Vosges you will pass a number of grand mansions (*hôtels particuliers*) which were occupied by the aristocracy in pre-Revolutionary times.

Belle Epoque (D 3-B 4)

The Grand Palais and the Petit Palais were built between the Champs-Elysées and the Seine for the 1900 World Exhibition. Cross the river at the Alexandre III bridge, then bear right and head for the Eiffel Tower.

Bohemian Paris (F 1-0)

Montmartre around the turn of the century provided inspiration for so many painters. Set off from Montmartre cemetery and climb up to the Place du Tertre via the Rue Lepic. Lose yourself in the maze of narrow streets, away from the crowds.

Paris is more than 2000 years old, and steeped in history. The city has played an important political role from Roman times right up to the present day. It has been the main stage not only for the key events in French history, but also for many important events which have influenced world history. The Ile de la Cité on the Seine is the historical centre of Paris. This was where the Celtic Parisii tribe first settled in around 300 BC. The strategically important settlement was colonized by Caesar during his conquest of Gaul in around 52 BC, and it was named Lutetia. During the 1st and 2nd centuries AD, the Romans rebuilt and fortified the settlement. They constructed public buildings, amphitheatres and baths, the remains of which can still be seen today.

Christianity began to take root in the 5th century. According to legend, Paris was saved from the Barbarians through the efforts of a devout Christian girl called Geneviève, who persuaded the Parisians not to flee Attila the Hun's marauding army. She was declared saviour of Paris and made patron saint of the city. By the end of the 5th century, the Christian king of the Franks, Clovis I, had finally driven the Romans out of Gaul and in 508 he declared Paris to be the capital of France. The city expanded further when it became the capital of the Western Frankish Empire around the year 1000.

During the Middle Ages, Paris became an important centre of learning and the church played a central role in its intellectual development. The city began to expand in the 12th and 13th centuries, when Notre-Dame and Sainte Chapelle were built and the Sorbonne university was founded.

During the Hundred Years' War (1339-1453), the English occupied France and the capital city at various different times. Henry VI of England was crowned King of France in Notre-Dame in 1430, but the English occupation of Paris came to an end in 1437. The endless battles had left the city in ruins, but prosperity gradually returned and with it renewed interest in art and architecture. The French kings were greatly influenced by the Italian Renaissance. François I, who ruled from 1515-1547, became

Bon Chic, Bon Genre

The upmarket districts, known as the Beaux Quartiers, lie in the west of the city. This is BCBG (pronounced bay-say-bay-jay) territory, where the safe conventional bourgeois style reigns. Bon chic, bon genre, basically means well groomed, 'well bred' and well off. He wears a tie, of course, English brogues, and designer jeans. In winter, a Loden coat and cashmere sweater. She wears a silk blouse, pearl necklace, handbag slung over one shoulder and around the neck, and a classic, understated hairstyle. Modest, decent and old-fashioned with expensive tastes. BCBG kids wear navy blue or grey. Other colours (and indeed anything else that stands out) are rejected as being just too vulgar for words.

known as the Renaissance king. He filled his court with artists and men of letters. It was he who brought Leonardo da Vinci and the *Mona Lisa* to France.

The 16th century saw an increase in religious tension. Protestants and Catholics engaged in bloody confrontations, which culminated in the St Bartholomew's Day massacre when about 3000 Protestant Huguenots were slain on 24 August 1572. In 1594 Henri IV, the foremost Protestant leader, converted to Catholicism, with the words *'Paris vaut bien une messe'* (Paris is well worth a mass). The city opened its gates to him, and from here Henri set about pacifying the country.

The reign of Louis XIV, the Sun King, (1643-1715) brought the greatest changes to the face of Paris. He ordered the construction of the palace of Versailles and of the two triumphal arches, Porte Saint-Denis and Porte Saint-Martin. He commissioned both the Hôtel des Invalides, to accommodate sick and wounded soldiers, and the Tuileries Gardens. He founded the Comédie Française, had his town planners design the Place des Victoires and the Place Vendôme and divided the city into districts or *arrondissements*. The increasing unrest felt by the poverty-stricken commoners under his successors led finally to the overthrow of the old order, the *Ancien Régime*. On 14 July 1789, the people of Paris stormed the Bastille, heralding the outbreak of revolution. Three years later the Republic was founded and on 21 January 1793 Louis XVI was beheaded.

The following years were turbulent. Thousands of people were killed on suspicion of betraying the Revolution, and the new government lacked stability. In 1799 Napoleon organized a *coup d'état* and seized power, and on 2 December 1804 he crowned himself Emperor in Notre-Dame. He established a new code of law, and ordered the construction of grand buildings and monuments. During his reign, Napoleon was continually at war until finally, in 1814, the Prussian and Russian troops occupied Paris and he was forced to abdicate.

In 1815 the monarchy was restored, but it didn't take long for civil unrest to grow again. The July Revolution of 1830 resulted in the establishment of a constitutional monarchy under the more liberal Louis Philippe. After the second revolution in 1848 the Second Republic was declared, but history repeated itself and in another *coup d'état* Napoleon's nephew defeated the Republic. In 1851 he declared the Second Empire and proclaimed himself Emperor Napoleon III. Over the next twenty years Paris quickly developed, and was transformed into a magnificent 19th-century metropolis, largely through the administration of Baron Haussmann, the Prefect of Paris.

In 1870, during the Franco-Prussian war, Bismarck's army defeated Napoleon III at Sedan. The Third Republic was immediately declared, but the Prussians soon laid siege to the capital and in May 1871 the Paris Commune was ruthlessly suppressed. Thousands were killed and much of the city was destroyed during the vicious fighting. But Paris quickly set about rebuilding itself and by the end of the century it was once more a prosperous and thriving city, its advancement proudly displayed to the world in the Universal Exhibitions of 1889 and 1900. This was a period of comfort and enjoyment, during which Paris was at the centre of the art world.

The outbreak of the First World War brought the Belle Epoque (the beautiful age) to an abrupt end. The German troops came to within 50 km of Paris, but didn't succeed in capturing it. During the Second World War, however, the Nazis succeeded in occupying the city from June 1940 until its liberation by the Allied forces in August 1944. France's Fourth Republic was established in 1946, and in 1958 Charles de Gaulle was elected President, marking the beginning of the Fifth Republic.

Wherever you look or walk, you will be surrounded by evidence of this rich and turbulent history. Take the view from the tower of Notre-Dame, for example. From this vantage point, you get a clear picture of the city's origins and subsequent development. From the modest foundations of the fishing village on this island on the Seine, the Romans built a city which extended along both banks of the river. Some indications of the ancient Roman settlement can still be seen today around the Latin Quarter. You can visit the former palaces of the Kings of France, such as the Conciergerie, the Louvre and the Palais du Luxembourg – not forgetting, of course, Versailles, the most magnificent example of the splendour epitomized by the Sun King, Louis XIV.

The places of key significance during the French Revolution are also of interest. Crucial events were played out in the Tuileries Gardens, and in the Place de la Concorde, where Louis XVI and many others were guillotined. Both of these places look much the same as they did during the Revolution, but it's a different story with the Bastille prison itself. With the exception of a few stones, visible from the métro, and a couple of exhibits in the Carnavalet museum, no traces of the original building remain.

Just by walking around the different areas, you can see the ways in which Paris has developed over the centuries. A simple journey on the métro takes you into the past. The route map reads like a roll-call of honour. You will pass stations named after battlefields like Wagram, Iéna and Austerlitz, Stalingrad and Bir-Hakeim, or after great statesmen like Richelieu and Charles de Gaulle. Once back at street level, you'll almost certainly come across one of the innumerable memorial plaques the Parisians are so fond of. The city is scattered with statues of historical figures, from Charlemagne to Georges Pompidou. History is everywhere – there's no getting away from it!

Paris is also the stage for all the major players in French politics. France's parliament, the National Assembly, is here; its impressive, columned façade visible from the Place de la Concorde across the Seine. The second parliamentary chamber, the Senate, meets in the Palais du Luxembourg, while the Elysée Palace, the President's residence, is just off the Champs-Elysées. Whenever you take a stroll down the exclusive Rue du Faubourg St-Honoré, lined with elegant shops, you are walking through the centre of power.

A number of important international institutions, like UNESCO and the OECD, have made Paris their home. Numerous international conferences, summit meetings and state visits are held here, and even the most disinterested tourist can't escape their presence completely. Barriers are regularly erected to cordon off various routes, while cavalcades of official cars are a common sight. The Gardes Républicaines, resplendent on horseback in their magnificent uniforms, the flags on show, the many firework displays, not to mention the frequent protest marches and demonstrations – these are all an integral part of the Parisian landscape.

Many of the ministries are located in the Faubourg St-Germain. The major exception is the Treasury, which is now housed in an enormous new building by the Seine to the east of Paris (Quai de Bercy). Ministers and officials had to quit the magnificent rooms in the wing of the Louvre that they used to occupy. The museum took over this wing and was thus able to increase the space available for its exhibits.

The many demonstrations – almost a daily occurrence in Paris – can be interesting to watch as they also illustrate certain aspects of politics which are peculiarly French. But the interested spectator should be aware that not all of these demonstrations are peaceful: if it should come to a violent confrontation, get out of the way quickly as neither side, once fired up, is likely to hold back!

Paris is a real haven for anyone with an interest in architecture, offering magnificent examples of all the major European styles covering a period of almost 2000 years, from Roman to post-modern. You can visit the remains of bathhouses and a circus arena dating from Roman times in the aptly named Latin Quarter. The baths can be found at the lower end of the Boulevard St-Michel, where it crosses the Boulevard St-Germain. The lovely Musée de Cluny, housed in a well-preserved medieval palace, is nearby. For Gothic architecture, Notre-Dame is a magnificent example of the movement at its most impressive, while the Sainte-Chapelle in the Palais de Justice is considered to be one of its most precious treasures. Renaissance and baroque styles in Paris have been given a particularly French expression – the beautiful aristocratic mansions in the Marais, the dome of Les Invalides, and the palace of Versailles, to name but a few, are inexhaustible sources of pleasure. Classicism is more strongly represented in Paris than in most other European cities, with the Panthéon, the Place de la Concorde and its surrounding buildings, and the Ecole Militaire among the most striking examples.

The fame which Paris enjoys today as a city of beauty and refinement can be traced back largely to the building developments of the 19th century, which still dominate the city landscape. This was the period when the great avenues and boulevards were laid out, admittedly destroying much of the medieval city in the process. Yet if it hadn't been for these changes, Paris would never have become the modern city it is today. We have the so-called Belle Epoque around the turn of the century to thank for the spectacular iron and glass structures, the prime examples being the Eiffel Tower and the métro – the 'city under the city'. Some of the original station entrances designed in the art nouveau style (or *style nouille* – 'noodle-style', as Parisians like to call it) are still in use today.

The 20th century brought with it a number of astonishing constructions, such as the church of Sacré-Coeur, the Palais de Chaillot with its echoes of Monumentalism, and, after the Second World War, a rash of towers of no immediately discernible purpose, the most prominent of which is the Tour Montparnasse, the second-highest tower in Europe. Le Corbusier, the leading light of French architecture at that time, didn't build much in Paris. However, it's worth visiting the Fondation Corbusier in the Square du Docteur-Blanche in the 16th *arrondissement.* The Rue Mallet-Stevens, where the houses were built in accordance with Mallet-Stevens art deco designs, is also in this district.

The mid-1950s saw the construction of the remarkable UNESCO building. Designed in the shape of a 'Y' resting on pillars, it is a striking building. A number of satellite towns developed during the post-war period. Some of these, such as Marne-la-Vallée, with its innovative housing projects, are worth visiting.

The developments in the Les Halles district continue to anger Parisians and incite vociferous protest. The old market halls were sadly pulled down and replaced with huge underground

L'Arche de la Défense, over 100 m tall, is the symbol of modern Paris

shopping centres and monstrous, soulless buildings. It's as well to remember, however, the initial horror expressed at the unveiling of the controversial cultural centre, the Centre Georges Pompidou (or Centre Beaubourg), with its 'high-tech' style and the 'innards' of the building deliberately exposed. The coloured pipework which snakes around the glass framework is now one of the first sights eager tourists look forward to seeing. Today, the structure is universally acclaimed and its impact is clearly shown by the crowds who flock there every day. The Centre has had a positive effect on the whole district and now enjoys a symbolic status.

Parisians have long harboured mixed feelings towards the high-rise district of La Défense, visible from Paris along an extension of the Champs-Elysées axis. No such ambiguity, however, for the latest architectural wonder there, the Arche de la Défense, which has attracted almost universal praise. This colossal construction is an open cube, about 110 m high, and is the work of the Danish architect von Spreckelsen. It has become as much a symbol of modern Paris as the Eiffel Tower has been for the past century.

The new Opéra at the Place de la Bastille must also be included in any discussion about the massive construction developments which have taken place over the last few years. With its glass and concrete façade dominating the surroundings, the building is controversial. That is only to be expected in a city like Paris however. Another example of the modern development which is carrying Paris into the 21st century is the Cité des Sciences et de l'Industrie at La Villette in the north-east of the city. This is an amazing, truly futuristic, city park with some astonishing buildings. The glass pyramid designed by the Chinese-American architect Ieoh Ming Pei has also achieved worldwide renown. This pyramid in the courtyard of the Louvre, with the modern entrance hall beneath it, is an impressive addition to the already considerable attractions of the museum. A recent addition to the townscape is the Bibliothèque François Mitterand, the national library, which has given the east side of Paris a facelift.

Then, of course, there is the Paris of fiction. What visitor has not, even unwittingly, followed in the footsteps of Hemingway? 'There are many ways of getting from the top of the Rue Cardinal-Lemoine down to the river… beyond the arm of the Seine lies the Ile St-Louis with its narrow streets, its tall, ancient and alluring houses… or you could turn left and walk along the Quais, tracing the outline of the Ile St-Louis and Notre-Dame… ' – across the Ile de la Cité and into the bookshop Shakespeare and Company, or to the Closerie des Lilas, where he had a regular spot at the bar. Many of the tables have little brass plaques which bear the names of well-known writers who were regulars – Max Jacob, André Breton, August Strindberg, James Joyce, Lenin, Paul Verlaine, Charles Baudelaire and Stéphane Mallarmé. If you carry on just a bit farther, you will come to the Carrefour Vavin, the heart of Montparnasse. Here you can see Rodin's imposing nightgowned figure of Balzac, which aroused so much adverse comment. Not far away, the Montparnasse cemetery is the final resting place of Jean-Paul Sartre, Simone de Beauvoir, Charles Baudelaire and Guy de Maupassant.

To continue in the literary vein, make your way to St-Germain-des-Prés and the Cafés de Flore, the Deux Magots and the long-established Procope, which was a watering hole for all the leading thinkers and writers in Paris even in pre-revolutionary times. You can still see Voltaire's old writing desk there. Visit the scenes of the turbulent relationship between Quasimodo and the beautiful Esmeralda, then have a look at the house of their creator, Victor Hugo, in the splendid Place des Vosges. Take a break in the 'enchanted' Palais Royal park, and dip into the works of Colette or Jean Cocteau who lived here. Call in at one of Balzac's residences and admire the legendary coffee pot, without which *La Comédie Humaine,* with its unsurpassed descriptions of Parisian life, might never have been written.

Exploring the city

Sweeping avenues, imposing palaces,
manicured gardens and hidden haunts

One of the best ways by far to explore the city is on foot. This is not as arduous as it sounds, because Paris without the suburbs – that is, the central part of most interest to visitors – is not all that big. With the help of the major landmarks easily visible from most parts of the city – the Eiffel Tower to the west, Notre-Dame in the centre, Sacré-Coeur to the north etc. – it won't take you long to find your bearings. When planning your itinerary, however, it pays to be selective. After all, you can't see everything, and relaxing over a coffee watching the world go by on the terrace of a café or bistro can prove more interesting than, say, a visit to the Conciergerie. Taking in the view of the rooftops of Paris from the steps of Sacré-Coeur at dusk is a thousand times more rewarding than trying to fight your way through the mass of tourists thronging the Place du Tertre only a few steps away.

Despite the recent closure of the Pompidou Centre for refurbishment, the forecourt is as lively as ever

There are plenty of Parisians who have never set foot in Les Invalides or taken a trip on one of the pleasure-boats which ferry tourists up and down the Seine. Many of the residents of the more upmarket districts in the west of the city have never ventured into the lively and colourful working-class district of Belleville, for example. They seem like two separate worlds, even though they are only a few métro stops apart. Then again, some Parisians never set foot inside the métro, although they are certainly missing out on something. The underground system is a 'city beneath a city' and a trip on the métro can be a fascinating experience in itself. You can catch some interesting views of the city from certain sections, especially if you take the lines between Charles de Gaulle-Etoile and Nation. Line 2 describes an arc across the northern districts, while line 6 covers the southern area. Though they may not provide the quickest connections, both these lines can be recommended because large stretches of the route run above ground and even above the traffic.

Another good way of exploring Paris is to use the public buses run by the Paris transport company RATP. It is generally a very efficient network and is good for short trips, although it is probably best avoided during the rush hour. A number of private companies run guided bus tours of the city (see page 92). These are usually good value and a good way to get your bearings.

Alternatively you could do some sightseeing by boat on a *vedette* or one of the giant pleasure cruisers known as *bateaux mouches*. They are fitted with powerful floodlights and also operate romantic evening tours. Many of the city's major landmarks are visible from the Seine, which runs right through the heart of Paris dividing it into the left and right bank. It's the perfect opportunity to see the beautiful bridges at close quarters.

Arc de Triomphe (B 2)

This grand triumphal arch stands proudly at the upper end of the Champs-Elysées and is a national symbol for the French. It was commissioned by Napoleon and dedicated to the glory of his imperial armies. He did not survive to see the finished monument, which wasn't completed until 1836 during the reign of the last French king, Louis Philippe. The arch is decorated with four large reliefs, each representing a key historic event: the 'Departure of the Army in 1792' (also called *La Marseillaise,* the title of the national anthem), the 'Triumph of Napoleon in 1810', the 'Resistance of 1814', and the 'Peace of 1815'. The mortal remains of both Napoleon (1840) and Victor Hugo (1885) lie in state beneath

MARCO POLO SELECTION: SIGHTSEEING

the monument. The Tomb of the Unknown Soldier was placed here in 1920, where an eternal flame burns to commemorate the dead of both wars. The Allies in 1918, the German Wehrmacht in 1940, and Charles de Gaulle after the Liberation in 1944, all staged military parades here. Today it is still the starting point for the Bastille Day parade. The view from the top of the 50 m high monument is one of the finest in Paris. You can see the Grande Arche de la Défense on one side and look down the Champs-Elysées to the Louvre on the other. The Place de l'Etoile is so-called because of the 12 avenues that radiate out from the arch in the form of a star (*l'étoile*). *Tues-Sat 10.00-22.30, Sun-Mon 10.00-18.00; Entrance 35 FF; Place de l'Etoile-Charles de Gaulle (8th arr.); Métro: Etoile*

Bibliothèque Nationale de France (F. Mitterand) (O)

Designed by Dominique Perrault, the new national library is vast. It comprises four L-shaped glass towers which are meant to resemble open books. They surround a wonderful tranquil space planted with pine trees. Very modern and striking.
Daily (except Mon) 10.00-19.00, Sun 12.00-18.00; 11, Quai François Mauriac (13th arr.); Métro: Quai de la Gare

Catacombs (O)

91 steps take you down into this underground necropolis, where you come face to face with the rather macabre inscription '*Arrête, c'est ici l'empire des Morts*' ('Stop, this is the empire of the dead'). The bones of around one million dead are kept here, brought from other cemeteries in the city which were closed because of the constant fear of infection. It's quite chilly inside the catacombs, so remember to bring an extra layer if you're dressed for warm weather.
Daily (except Mon and public holidays) 14.00-16.00, Sat/Sun 09.00-11.00 and 14.00-16.00; Entrance 27 FF; 2, Place Denfert Rochereau (14th arr.); Métro: Denfert Rochereau

Eiffel Tower (B 4)

★ ☁ Designed by the engineer Gustave Eiffel (1832-1923) to commemorate the centenary of the Revolution, the tall, graceful iron tower, which only took two years to build, was inaugurated on 6 May 1889. 7175 tonnes of iron were used in its construction and at 300 m it was then the tallest building in the world. Initially the structure wasn't at all well received. Eiffel was mercilessly scorned and accused of completely destroying the Paris skyline. However, it wasn't long

Every year nearly six million people visit the Eiffel Tower

before it became internationally famous and has been the city's definitive landmark ever since. The Eiffel Tower may be over 100 years old and a bit rusty around the edges, but modern lifts and a spectacular system of spotlighting have done much to enhance the beauty of the 'grand old lady'. More than five and a half million people come here each year, so there's always a queue to get in. The restaurant offers both good-quality food and a great view.

Daily 09.30-23.00; Entrance: 1st floor 20 FF, 2nd floor 42 FF, 3rd floor 57 FF; children under 12 half-price, stairs as far as 2nd floor 14 FF; Quai Branly (7th arr.); Métro: Bir Hakeim, Ecole Militaire, Trocadéro

La Grande Arche de la Défense (O)

★ ◁▷ Designed by the Danish architect von Spreckelsen and opened in 1989, this unique construction can be regarded as both a city gate and the end point of the long axis running from the Place de la Bastille via the Louvre, the Champs-Elysées and the Arc de Triomphe. An open-sided cube of white marble, the pure clarity of its form and its immense size make it one of the most impressive sights in the city. At 110 m, it is more than twice the height of the Arc de Triomphe. Even Notre-Dame would fit comfortably underneath it. If it's not too busy, it only takes a few seconds to reach the top in the glass panoramic lift. From here, you get an amazing view of the surrounding high-rise business district of La Défense, central Paris and the western suburbs.

Daily 09.00-19.00; Panoramic lift to viewing platform: 40 FF; Métro: Grande Arche de la Défense

Ile de la Cité (F-G 4-5)

It was on this island in the Seine that the first inhabitants of Paris settled during the 3rd century BC. Apart from the cathedral, the main attractions here are the Conciergerie, the Palais de Justice, Sainte-Chapelle and Place Dauphine. A good starting point for a walking tour of the island is the western tip at the Pont Neuf. From here, you can walk across the Place Dauphine, along the bank of the Seine and over to Notre-Dame. Although there are a few old houses near the cathedral, much of the island's medieval character was lost during the extensive rebuilding that took place in the 19th century. The triangular Place Dauphine was laid out by Henri IV and was originally surrounded by three rows of houses. The square has retained much of its charm and is a peaceful romantic spot. (Yves Montand and Simone Signoret lived here.) There is a pretty flower and bird market by the Préfecture de Police. The Conciergerie is the only part of the old Royal Palace dating from the 13th century to survive. During the Reign of Terror those condemned to death were held prisoner inside the damp, dark vaults of the building, and the dungeons where Marie-Antoinette and many other prisoners awaited their fate are still a chilling sight.

Daily (except public holidays) 10.00-17.00; Entrance 32 FF; 1, Quai de l'Horloge (1st arr.); Métro: Cité

Ile St-Louis (G-H 5)

★ Connected to the Ile de la Cité by a pedestrian bridge (a favourite busking and skateboarding spot) the other island on the Seine is like a separate world. Its narrow streets are lined with wonderful 17th century residences, and it is one of the most exclusive areas to live in Paris. As you wander around the island you'll come across a variety of commercial galleries, restaurants and smart shops alongside picture-postcard scenes of painters and lovers beneath the plane trees and poplars that line the banks of the Seine. *Métro: Pont Marie (4th arr.)*

Invalides   (D 4)
The area is named after the vast Hôtel des Invalides built by Louis XIV as a home for disabled and wounded soldiers. The complex is dominated by the imposing 107 m high golden dome, a masterpiece of French baroque architecture which has recently been restored to its former glory. The façade, on the other hand, is strictly classical. You can see into the dome from the church of St-Louis-des-Invalides. Most visitors come here to see Napoleon's tomb, but for those with an interest in military history there is also an Army Museum (see page 38). *Daily 10.00-17.00 (until 19.00 in winter); Entrance 37 FF; Place Vauban (7th arr.); Métro: Latour Maubourg, Varenne, Invalides*

Métro
❂ This is not only the quickest, cheapest and safest way of getting about, the Paris Métro is also worth seeing as a place of interest in its own right. It is virtually a city beneath the city and, with more than 200 km of tunnels and over 300 stations, carries more than 4 million passengers daily. The first line was opened in 1900 between Porte de Vincennes and

Porte Maillot. Unfortunately, only a few of the original art nouveau entrances designed by the architect Hector Guimard remain intact. The best examples can be seen at the Abbesses and Porte Dauphine stations. The largest and busiest underground station in the world is Châtelet-Les Halles. It serves Beaubourg and the shopping and leisure complex of the Forum des Halles. Forum No. 2 has countless shops and boutiques, a swimming pool, an oceanarium, a cinema complex, and a *vidéothèque* – a museum where every film either shot in Paris or about Paris is stored and screened.

Palais de l'Elysée   (D 2)
Built in the 17th century, the Elysée Palace is to Paris what the White House is to Washington DC. Madame de Pompadour lived here from 1721-64. After the Revolution, Napoleon made considerable changes to the palace and it was here that he abdicated following the battle of Waterloo in 1815. The Elysée Palace has been home to the Presidents of France for over 100 years and during the 5th Republic it became the real centre of power. Although visits are not permitted you can get a good view from the gate at the Rue du Faubourg-St-Honoré. The cabinet meets every Wednesday. *55, Rue du Faubourg-St-Honoré (8th arr.); Métro: Champs-Elysées Clémenceau*

Palais and Jardin du Luxembourg   (F 5-6)
✥ ❂ Marie de' Medici, the widow of Henri IV, commissioned this small Italianate palace to remind

her of her Tuscan home. It was built in the early 17th century and its design was modelled on the Pitti Palace in Florence. Originally the walls were decorated with 24 paintings by Rubens based on the life of the queen; these now hang in the Louvre. Today the Palais du Luxembourg is the seat of the Senate, the second parliamentary chamber.

The Jardin du Luxembourg is the most popular place on the Left Bank to relax in. The park's many attractions include the Fontaine de Médicis, numerous statues, an open air café, a merry-go-round and puppet theatre, boules and chess playing areas, tennis courts, and even beehives. The gardens are closed at night.

Métro: Odéon, Luxembourg (6th arr.)

Jardin du Luxembourg: an oasis of peace beyond the busy Latin Quarter

Palais and Jardin du Palais Royal (F 3)

★ Cardinal Richelieu had his residence built next to the Louvre Palace in 1629. Later the building was taken over by Philippe II of Orléans, brother of Louis XIV. Under his occupancy the palace became a notorious centre for gambling and debauchery. With the subsequent setting up of apartments, shops, galleries and the Comédie Française (France's national theatre), the Palais Royal became a favourite meeting place. The intellectuals who gathered here regularly were among those who helped prepare the way for the French Revolution, and it was from here that the first call to arms was heard in 1789. Today the palace is occupied by the Ministry of Culture. The courtyard is now decorated with the controversial Colonnes de Buren; a modern sculpture made up of black and white columns of varying heights. A stone's throw away from the busy Avenue de l'Opéra, the palace gardens, lined with small boutiques and restaurants, are a haven of peace in the heart of Paris.

Place du Palais Royal (1st arr.); Métro: Palais Royal

Panthéon (G 5)

This imposing neo-classical building dominates the Latin Quarter. The massive 83 m-high dome is supported by columns and weighs nearly 10 000 tonnes. It was commissioned by Louis XV who intended it to be a mausoleum for the remains of Sainte Geneviève, patron saint of Paris. It wasn't completed until 1790. After the Revolution, it was decided that the Panthéon should house the tombs of the great and the good: Emile Zola and Rousseau are among their number. There were construction difficulties with the huge building right from the start and repairs are continuously being carried out.

Daily 10.00-18.00; Entrance 32 FF; Place du Panthéon (5th arr.); Métro: Luxembourg

The Sewers (Les Egouts) (C 3)

Although the idea may not sound very appealing, the Paris sewers are a popular tourist attraction. They were built in the 19th century by Haussmann and, if laid end to end, the labyrinth of tunnels would stretch for more than 2000 km. The small section open to the public is beneath the Quai d'Orsay. As you might expect, the atmosphere is pretty musty and the paths can be slippery, but it doesn't feel at all claustrophobic because the sewers themselves are surprisingly large. A film explains how the system works.

Daily (except Thurs/Fri) 11.00-17.00; Entrance 24 FF; Pont de l'Alma corner of the Quai d'Orsay (7th arr.); Métro: Alma Marceau

UNESCO Building (C 5)

The building which houses the Unesco (United Nations Educational, Scientific and Cultural Organization) headquarters was designed in 1958 by the architects Zehrfuss, Breuer and Nervi. It is built in the shape of a wide open 'Y', the main section of which rests on pillars. Because the façade is largely of glass, the whole structure has a light and airy effect. You can get a good view of the layout from the top of the nearby Eiffel Tower. Outside in the forecourt there is a sculpture by Henry Moore and a giant black metal mobile designed by Alexander Calder. A number of famous artists contributed to the interior design, among them Picasso, who painted a mural, Miró who designed the ceramics, and Le Corbusier.

Mon-Fri 09.00-17.00; Main entrance 7, Place de Fontenoy (7th arr.); Métro: Ségur, Cambronne

Versailles (O)

★ Louis XIV, the Sun King, had a lifelong passion for building palaces and laying out formal gardens, and used a large part of the state's finances to realize these ambitions. The French monarchy was at the height of its power in the late 17th century and Versailles was its most glorious expression. The whole court consisted of 20 000 people who periodically held residence here, not to mention the 35 000 workers with 6000 horses who were required just to maintain the vast enterprise. You need at least a whole day to do justice to Versailles, and the beautifully landscaped park and formal gardens are seen at their best in the spring and autumn. Outdoor concerts held on summer Sundays are an added attraction.Winter is also a good time to visit because the formal landscape of terraces, parterres, pools, statues and fountains can be seen even more clearly. Most people don't have time to see everything. Priority should be given to the Chapel, the State Rooms and the 75-m long Hall of Mirrors, all of which can be seen without a guide. There are guided tours (in French and English) for the rest of the palace. Unfortunately, Versailles is always crowded, so it's best to get there as early as possible. The Grand and Petit Trianons, the smaller palaces in the park, are also well worth seeing.

Palace open daily (except Mon, 1 May and 25 Dec) 09.00-17.30 (until 19.00 in summer); Entrance 45FF; Park: from sunrise to sunset; Fountain displays on 1st, 3rd and 4th Sun of each month from May to Oct; Entrance 20 FF; Grand and Petit

Trianons: 09.45-12.00 and 14.00-17.00; Entrance 25 FF; Bus tours (Cityrama): daily all-day or half-day trips, Tel. 01 42 60 30 14; Cost 165 and 265 FF; RER: all C-Line stations on Left Bank: Gare d'Austerlitz, St Michel, Invalides, Champ de Mars and Javel. Or Gare St Lazare to Versailles-Rive-Droite, every 15 minutes; Gare Montparnasse to Versailles-Chantier-Rive-Gauche; RATP bus, No. 171 from Pont de Sèvres

AVENUES

Avenue des Champs-Elysées (C-D 2-3)

The Champs-Elysées runs from the Place de la Concorde to the Arc de Triomphe/Place Charles de Gaulle and is almost 2 km long. The elegant lower section as far as Rond-Point is lined with trees, lawns, restaurants and one or two theatres. The upper section between Rond-Point and the Arc de Triomphe is fenced in by a number of imposing buildings. Once an elegant shopping street, in recent years the avenue has suffered under the strain of traffic and modern developments, with the explosion of cinemas, fast-food outlets and shopping malls. Nowadays the vast majority of people you see here are tourists or cinema-goers. The shops are expensive and not of particularly good quality, and the bars and bistros are often tourist traps. There are some notable exceptions, however, such as *Fouquet's* at the corner of Avenue George V.

To be fair, the Parisian authorities have at last begun to make an effort to restore the avenue to some of its former glory. The recent completion of a new underground car park is helping to ease the traffic congestion. The streets have been newly paved, trees have been planted and new café terraces opened, turning the Champs-Elysées once again into a pleasant, though crowded place to while away some time.

The more elegant streets surrounding the Champs-Elysées are lined with expensive fashion boutiques and plush offices. The avenue is particularly impressive at night, with the floodlit Arc de Triomphe at one end and Place de la Concorde at the other, especially when it is festooned with flags and tree-lights. Each year on Bastille Day (14 July) a military parade is held here in celebration of the French national holiday. The avenue is also the final stage of the Tour de France.

Métro: Charles de Gaulle-Etoile, George V, Franklin-D. Roosevelt, Concorde (8th arr.)

Avenue Foch (A-B 2)

'Millionaire's Row' runs from the Place de l'Etoile to the Bois de Boulogne. At the western end of the avenue you'll find one of the few remaining art nouveau métro stations, Porte Dauphine.

Métro: Charles de Gaulle-Etoile, Porte Dauphine (16th arr.)

Avenue Montaigne (C-D 3)

One of the smartest streets in Paris, the Avenue Montaigne runs between Champs-Elysées Rond-Point and Place de l'Alma. It is the centre of Parisian haute couture. Just about every famous couturier and up-and-coming designer has a boutique here. The legendary Plaza Athénée hotel is at no. 25.

Métro: Franklin-D. Roosevelt, Alma Marceau (8th arr.)

Relax and enjoy the view of the city from the terrace café at the top of 'La Samaritaine' department store

BRIDGES

Pont Alexandre III (D 3)

This magnificent bridge, with its elaborate lamps and golden statues, is the widest in Paris. It spans 108 m connecting the Esplanade des Invalides on the Left Bank with the Petit Palais and Grand Palais on the Right Bank. It was opened in 1900 for the Universal Exhibition and was named after Tsar Alexander III, with whom France was allied at the time.
Métro: Invalides (7th/8th arr.)

Pont des Arts (F 4)

This iron footbridge just west of the Pont Neuf was built in 1803/4. It offers lovely views over the Ile de la Cité. An especially romantic spot at sunset.
Métro: Pont Neuf, Louvre Rivoli

Pont Neuf (F 4)

The Pont Neuf (new bridge) is in fact the oldest of the Seine's bridges. It was inaugurated in 1606 by Henri IV whose eques-

trian statue stands in the central section, opposite the Place Dauphine on the Ile de la Cité. Behind the monument, a flight of steps leads down to a small park, the Square du Vert-Galant. In the 17th and 18th centuries the bridge was used for popular entertainments and festivities. Today you can sit and enjoy the view of the river and the buildings along the *quais* from the stone benches that have been placed at intervals along the bridge. In 1985 the Bulgarian artist Christo wrapped the entire structure in sandstone-coloured fabric – a memorable event which put the bridge back on the map and drew Parisians to look at it with renewed appreciation.
Métro: Pont Neuf (1st/6th arr.)

CANALS

(E4-O) The boat trip along the tree-lined canal St-Martin is a pleasant excursion. Cruises depart from the Musée d'Orsay or Bastille

(Porte de l'Arsenal) and end at the Bassin de la Villette.

Duration 3 hours; Paris Canal Co.: Tel. 01 42 40 96 97; Canauxrama: Tel. 01 42 39 15 00; Departure: 13, Quai de la Loire; Métro: Jaurès

CEMETERIES

Cimetière de Montmartre   (O)
This cemetery near Pigalle has a romantic, rather eerie atmosphere. Among its many picturesque gravestones are those of the painters Fragonard (whose tombstone is an artist's palette), Utrillo and Degas, the German poet Heinrich Heine, French writers Stendhal and Zola (whose actual remains are in the Panthéon) and composers Berlioz and Offenbach. *La Dame aux Camélias,* Alphonsine Plessis, the courtesan immortalized by Alexandre Dumas in his eponymous novel, is also buried here.

Daily 09.00-17.30; Avenue Rachel (18th arr.); Métro: Blanche, Place de Clichy

Cimetière de Montparnasse   (E 6)
★ This cemetery was laid out in 1824. Among the many artists, scientists and literary figures buried here are Jean-Paul Sartre, Simone de Beauvoir, Baudelaire, Guy de Maupassant, Antoine Bourdelle, Ossip Zadkine, Constantin Brancusi and Serge Gainsbourg. You can obtain a map of the grounds at the main entrance.

Daily 09.00-17.30; Bd Edgar-Quinet (14th arr.); Métro: Edgar Quinet

Père Lachaise   (O)
✣ The largest cemetery in Paris, Père Lachaise, with its little cobbled lanes lined with graves is like a miniature town. The site was originally occupied by Louis XIV's confessor, the Jesuit priest François de la Chaise d'Aix. The land was bought by Napoleon who turned the hill into a burial ground. The cemetery is filled with beautifully ornate gravestones, sculptures and mausoleums and is a wonderful place to stroll in. It's a good idea to ask for a map of the grounds at the main entrance, not only to find your way around but also to read the impressive list of occupants. Among the many famous names are Dr Guillotine, inventor of the instrument of execution, Molière, La Fontaine, Haussmann, Balzac, Apollinaire, Marcel Proust, Edith Piaf, Jim Morrison, Oscar Wilde, Sarah Bernhardt, Chopin and Colette. It was here, in 1871, that the last members of the Paris Commune were shot and buried together in a mass grave.

Daily 08.30-17.00; 16, Rue du Repos (20th arr.); Métro: Père Lachaise, Gambetta

CHURCHES

Madeleine   (E 2)
Napoleon had this memorial church built in 1806 to honour his army. The design of the building was based on Greek principles of architecture, hence the 52 Corinthian columns which surround the main section. The interior is not as impressive as the exterior, however. Many a high-society wedding is held here.

Daily 08.30-19.00; Place de la Madeleine (8th arr.); Métro: Madeleine

Notre-Dame   (G 5)
★ ◁▷ A masterpiece of Gothic architecture, Notre-Dame has featured in countless novels and

films and is virtually a history of France in stone. Kings, queens and even an emperor – Napoleon – have been crowned here. During the Revolution, the cathedral was dedicated to the 'highest being' and declared a Temple of Reason. Later the writer Victor Hugo put the building on the world map by using it as the setting for his classic novel *The Hunchback of Notre-Dame.*

Building of the cathedral began in 1163 but was not completed until the mid-14th century. The façade with its three portals, two squat towers and central stained-glass rose window is a spectacular sight. It is worth climbing the 387 steps up to the 68-m high north tower for the panorama over the rooftops of Paris and the close-up view of the gargoyles. The treasury which houses ancient religious treasures is also open to the public. Organ concerts are held here on Sunday afternoons.

Tower: daily 10.00-17.00; Entrance 32 FF; Place du Parvis-Notre-Dame (4th arr.); Métro: Cité

Sacré-Coeur (O)

☙ This striking building, which dominates the northern skyline of Paris, was built towards the end of the 19th century. It was conceived as a symbol of reconciliation and an expression of patriotic renewal after the traumatic events of the Franco-Prussian War (1870-71) and the Paris Commune. Dedicated in 1919, the Romano-Byzantine dome has become as much a feature of the Parisian skyline as the Eiffel Tower. The interior is not especially interesting, but prayers have been said here round-the-clock for over 100 years, day and

The gleaming white domes of the Sacré-Coeur are visible from afar

night. The hill on which it stands, Montmartre, is about 130 m high and the view from the top is breathtaking at night, when Paris is laid out like a sea of light. If you feel up to it, you can climb the 237 steps to the top of the dome of Sacré-Coeur and you'll be rewarded with a stunning view of the romantic alleys and hidden gardens of Montmartre.

Dome: 10.00-17.00, summer 09.00-18.00; a cable car runs from the Marché St-Pierre to Sacré-Coeur; Parvis-du-Sacré-Coeur (18th arr.); Métro: Anvers

St-Denis (O)

The church of Saint-Denis is in one of the northern suburbs but can be reached quite easily on métro line 13 or with the RER D line. This Gothic church was the model for many other churches in France and although it has often been damaged and plundered, it has always been lovingly restored. This was the preferred final resting place for many French monarchs, and the Royal

Crypt is one of the best examples of medieval and Renaissance French memorial art.

Daily (except public holidays) 10.00-17.00, from 12.00 on Sun; Entrance to crypt: 32 FF; Métro: St-Denis-Basilique; RER: D St-Denis

St-Etienne-du-Mont　　　　(G 5)

This splendid church is a mixture of Renaissance and Gothic design. It is the burial place of Sainte Geneviève, patron saint of Paris, who saved the city from destruction by Attila the Hun in the 5th century. The remains of two literary giants – Racine and Pascal – also lie here.

Daily 08.00-12.00 and 14.00-19.30; Place du Panthéon (5th arr.); Métro: Cardinal Lemoine, Maubert Mutualité; RER: Luxembourg

St-Eustache　　　　(G 3)

One of the most beautiful churches in Paris, St-Eustache has no tower but displays a remarkable mixture of styles on its façade. The interior is a combination of Gothic and Renaissance. The acoustics are impressive, as are the stained-glass windows. There are a number of frescos, and a painting by Rubens hangs alongside the grave of Colbert. The restored organ, boasting 7000 pipes, is magnificent. Organ and jazz concerts are held regularly here, usually on Wednesdays at 18.30.

Daily 08.00-19.00; 1, Rue du Jour (1st arr.); Métro: Les Halles

St-Germain-des-Prés　　　　(F 4)

This is the oldest church in Paris, dating from the 11th century. There was also a thriving monastic community here in the 8th century, but unfortunately little physical evidence of this survives today. Descartes is buried here.

Daily 07.30-19.45, Mon from 12.30; 3, Place St-Germain-des-Prés (6th arr.); Métro: St-Germain-des-Prés

Sainte-Chapelle　　　　(G 4)

This jewel of Gothic architecture lies hidden behind the walls of the Palais de Justice on the Ile de la Cité. The chapel, which dates from the 13th century, is the earliest surviving section of the former Royal Palace. The blue and gold lower section was allocated to the servants for worship, while the upper section, the Sainte-Chapelle itself, with its magnificent stained-glass windows, was reserved for the royal court.

Daily (except public holidays) summer 09.30-18.30, winter 10.00-17.00; Entrance 32 FF; Boulevard du Palais (1st arr.); Métro: Cité

DISTRICTS

Bastille　　　　(H-I 4-5)

★ ♟ Until recently a predominantly working-class area, Bastille has developed over the last few years into a trendy district, full of artists and young people who can no longer afford the prices of the Marais and Left Bank. It is often likened to Montmartre at the turn of the century or Montparnasse in the 1920s. For centuries the area was renowned for its furniture makers; now it is full of art dealers and galleries. Nothing remains of the legendary prison which once stood by the Place de la Bastille apart from a few pieces of the old wall which you can see in the métro station. The large column in the middle of the square was built as a memorial to the victims of the July Revolution of 1830 and the 1848 uprising. The square is now dominated by the Opéra de la Bastille which was opened in 1989 on the bicentennial of Bastille Day. The façade of the new building has been the subject of some controversy, but there is no doubting the technical expertise needed to build it. There are lots of bars, bistros and night-clubs in the streets around the square. The trendy nightspots are concentrated around the Rue de Lappe and Rue de la Roquette.

The Place d'Aligre is a lively spot and well worth a visit. A small market sells fresh vegetables, spices and other goods, and the neighbouring streets support a fair number of restaurants and bistros. Wine from the barrel is on offer at *Le Baron Rouge, 1, Rue Théophile Roussel. Vegetable and flea market: Daily (except Mon) 09.00-13.00; Métro: Bastille, Faidherbe Chaligny, Ledru Rollin (11th/12th arr.)*

Belleville (I 2)

❂ Not much is left of the original architecture and atmosphere of this legendary working-class district, where Edith Piaf and Maurice Chevalier once sang in seedy nightclubs. Belleville has suffered at the hands of the developers. It is now dominated by high-rise blocks and few of the original little terraced streets remain. Nevertheless it is a lively and colourful area. Immigrants from all over the world have settled here – North Africans, Eastern Europeans, West Indians and Asians – and it is full of interesting bars, shops, markets and ethnic restaurants. *Market on the Boulevard de Belleville: Tues and Fri am; Métro: Belleville (20th arr.)*

Chinatown (O)

Although it is known as 'Chinatown', the modern district of Olympiades with its skyscrapers and concrete blocks is actually home to large numbers of Vietnamese, Laotian and Cambodian as well as Chinese immigrants. There are lots of Asian restaurants and shops and the two supermarkets in the Avenue d'Ivry (*Tang at no. 48 and the Paris-Store at no. 44*) stock a remarkable range of Oriental foods and products. *Métro: Tolbiac (13th arr.)*

Les Halles and Beaubourg (G 3-4)

❂ ♟ Every day thousands of people pour out of the largest underground station in the world, Les Halles, most of them to visit the Forum 1 and Forum 2 shopping malls. Although these vast commercial centres don't offer anything out of the ordinary, they still attract hordes of people. Unfortunately very little remains of the old iron market pavilions, which were pulled down to make way for the modern complex. The park is pleasant enough, though it does attract down-and-outs, and offers a good view of St-Eustache, the imposing Gothic church next to the complex. In the surrounding streets you can still find traditional bistros and pubs which were here when the market halls still stood. The Rue Montorgueil with its colourful market and pleasant bistros has been transformed into an attractive pedestrian precinct. The Rue St-Denis, on the other hand, has become a bit of a tourist trap with its souvenir and sex shops and tacky bistros.

On the other side of the Boulevard de Sébastopol is Beaubourg,

Les Halles and St-Eustache

a lively and colourful district. Although a number of tourist pubs and souvenir shops have been established here, the district is still best known for the Pompidou Centre (unfortunately closed for refurbishment until 1 Jan 2000), as well as its galleries, art shops and fashion boutiques.
Métro: Châtelet Les Halles (1st arr.)

The Marais (H 3)

During the 17th century, this area was the domain of rich aristocrats. As other districts became more fashionable the grand town mansions they lived in were abandoned and fell into disrepair. The beauty of these buildings, however, has since been rediscovered and the whole area has undergone a complete facelift. Today the newly gentrified Marais is once more home to the wealthy. Most of the buildings are under preservation order, which means they are safe from unscrupulous developers. Apart from the numerous galleries, bistros, boutiques and cafés in the area, the main attractions here are the Musée Carnavalet and the Musée Picasso, the Jewish quarter around the Rue des Rosiers and the Place des Vosges. This square dates back to the reign of Henri IV when it was known as the Place Royale. It was here that Victor Hugo lived and wrote. The 17th century houses and arcades that surround the square have been restored to their former splendour. The manicured garden in the middle of the square is a lovely spot to relax in.
Métro: Bastille, St Paul (4th arr.)

Montmartre (F 1)

Montmartre can be divided into two separate areas. At the bottom of the hill the red-light district is centred around Place Pigalle and Place Blanche, dominated by garish neon signs, sex shops, strip clubs, bars and short-stay hotels. This is where you'll find the legendary Moulin-Rouge, where the cancan has been danced for tourists for over 100 years. With the re-emergence of discos, clubs and concert venues, Pigalle has more recently become a hot spot for Parisian night-owls.

As you start to make your way up to the Butte Montmartre the atmosphere changes. Around the turn of the century, the old village was the place for every self-respecting artist and bohemian to be. Renoir, Toulouse-Lautrec and Utrillo all lived here. Picasso, Juan Gris and Braque lived and worked in the *Bateau Lavoir* studios on the peaceful Place Emile-Goudeau. This was where Cubism and the modern movement took root. Picasso painted his *Demoiselles d'Avignon* here, and although the original studio burned down in 1970, it has since been fully restored. A number of narrow streets, alleyways and steps lead up the hill to the Sacré-Coeur. The best route up to Montmartre is to set off from Place Blanche, walk along the lively market street Rue Lepic, turn right into Rue des Abbesses, go through Place Emile-Goudeau, along Rue Ravignan, and climb the steps up to the church. If you're not feeling that energetic, you could always take the cable car from Marché St-Pierre. Unfortunately, the area around the Place du Tertre has developed into a tourist trap, swarming with amateur artists offering to paint your 'portrait'. But if you venture off the beaten track you can still find some pretty and relatively peaceful side streets and alleyways to explore.

Métro: Abbesses, Pigalle, Blanche (18th arr.)

Montparnasse   (E 6)

✪ The other artists' quarter on the left bank of the Seine became fashionable after the First World War, when Montmartre had become too over-crowded. Artists moved into studios here, and patronized the cafés around the Carrefour Vavin. Modigliani, van Dongen, Soutine, Chagall and Picasso were among them. Trotsky, Lenin and Hemingway were also regulars in the Closerie des Lilas. Man Ray photographed Kiki de Montparnasse in the Istria Hotel. Nowadays, Montparnasse is best known for the cinemas and restaurants concentrated on the Boulevard du Montparnasse. The whole area is dominated by the Tour Montparnasse which, at 209 m is the second tallest tower in Europe. For 42 FF you can take the lift to the observation platform on the 56th floor.

Métro: Vavin, Montparnasse Bien-venue (14th arr.)

Quartier Latin   (F-G 5)

✪ ✝ The Latin Quarter on the left bank of the Seine occupies most of the 5th and a part of the 6th *arrondissement,* where it runs into St-Germain-des-Prés. The university of the Sorbonne is here along with a number of other schools and academic institutes. The Sorbonne has been one of the great European seats of learning since medieval times, and today the district is still dominated by the university and the numerous cafés, bars and cinemas that cater mostly for students. The lower part of the Boulevard St-Michel is a popular meeting place for young people and is full of boutiques and bookshops. The pedestrian precinct around the Place St-Michel and the Rue de la Huchette, with its many cinemas, fast-food outlets and bistros, is always crowded. Things are a bit quieter further up towards the Panthéon, around the church of St-Etienne-du-Mont and Place de la Contrescarpe, a small tree-lined square at the upper end of the market street, Rue Mouffetard. The whole area offers a good choice of cafés and restaurants.

Métro: Odéon, Place Monge, Cardinal Lemoine (5th/6th arr.)

St-Germain-des-Prés   (E-F 4)

★ ✪ This district, once renowned as the intellectual and artistic mecca and centre of café culture on the Left Bank, is today better known for its antiques, hotels and sophisticated shops and restaurants. Many of the old bookshops had to make way for new cafés, discos, jazz venues and expensive fashion boutiques. In spite of its gentrification, however, the quarter has retained its soul and you

can still spend hours just wandering about the lovely old streets soaking up the atmosphere. The most renowned cafés in the area are the Café de Flore, Les Deux Magots, and Brasserie Lipp right by the church of St-Germain.
Métro: St-Germain-des-Prés (6th arr.)

La Villette (O)

🏃 This new park to the north-east of Paris is set in the former slaughterhouse district and is divided across the middle by a canal. In the 1980s the abattoir ruins within the park were converted into a vast arts and science museum (see page 40). Part of the old wrought iron cattle hall has been beautifully restored and is now used to stage exhibitions, concerts and plays. The park also contains the Zénith, a huge rock concert venue, and the spherical cinema known as La Géode, which projects special effects films on a vast screen. The ultra-modern Cité de la Musique is made up of a music school, museum and concert hall. A roofed walkway runs for one kilometre through the park which is dotted with geometric figures carved out of trees, lawns, gardens and the bright red so-called *folies* designed by architect Bernard Tschumi.
Daily (except Mon) 10.00-18.00, Parc La Villette (19th arr.); Métro: Porte de Pantin or Porte de la Villette

GALLERIES & ARCADES

The *passages*, glass-roofed shopping arcades with tiled floors and flamboyant décor, also known as *galeries*, enjoyed their heyday during the 19th century, before the appearance of large department stores. Most of these arcades were built around the *grands boulevards* in the 1st and 2nd *arrondissements*. The 20 or so which survived have, for the most part, been restored and are enjoying something of a revival.

Galerie Vivienne (F 3)

This light-filled shopping arcade with its marble floors is near the Place des Victoires. It has been wonderfully restored and is lined with tearooms, fashion boutiques (including Jean-Paul Gaultier), bookshops and antique dealers.
Rue des Petits Champs (2nd arr.); Métro: Bourse

Galerie Vivienne

Passage Colbert (F 3)

Next to the Galerie Vivienne, lavishly and elegantly renovated. Art books and Salon de thé.
Rue des Petits Champs (2nd arr.); Métro: Bourse

Passage des Panoramas (F 2)

The first gas lighting in Paris was installed in this arcade. Once a popular meeting place for high society people, drawn here by its

variety theatres, cafés, and luxury shops, the atmosphere today is more subdued. Near the Musée Grévin waxworks.
11, Boulevard Montmartre (2nd arr.); Métro: Richelieu Drouot

Passage-Galerie Véro-Dodat (F 3)

Antiques and dolls. Old-fashioned, but enchanting.
19, Rue Jean-Jacques Rousseau (1st arr.); Métro: Les Halles

GRANDS BOULEVARDS

❧ Parisians still love to stroll along the wide tree-lined *grands boulevards* which run from the church of the Madeleine to the Place de la République. They were initially laid out during the reign of Louis XIV, over the remains of the demolished city walls. The two arches at Porte St-Denis and Porte St-Martin, once the gateways to the city, also date from this time. The boulevards only really came into their own during the 19th century, when they were lined by elegant mansions in the more refined western districts. To the east, the boulevards were filled with theatres, ballrooms, cafés and restaurants. Many of the former theatres were later turned into cinemas.

PARKS & GARDENS

Bois de Boulogne (O)

❧ The 900 hectare Bois de Boulogne lies in the west of the city. This huge stretch of parkland is a popular place for strolling, dog-walking, jogging and picnicking. You can go boating on a lake, eat in one of the restaurants, or spend a day at the Longchamp racecourse. There is an activity park for children (Jardin d'Acclimatation), and a wonderful rose garden in the Parc de Bagatelle.
Métro: Porte Maillot, Porte d'Auteuil, Pont de Neuilly; Bus: No.43 to terminus

Bois de Vincennes (O)

❧ The 'green lung' in the east of the city boasts a racecourse, a flower garden, three lakes and a theatre, run by the Théâtre du Soleil, set in a converted factory. The park also houses the largest zoo in Paris. If you're feeling in an active mood, you can hire a bike or go boating on Lac Daumesnil. Very popular for family outings, particularly on Sundays.
Mon-Fri 09.00-17.00, Sat/Sun 09.00-18.30; Entrance 40 FF, children 20 FF; Métro: St-Mandé Tourelle, Porte Dorée (12th arr.)

Jardin des Plantes and Musée National d'Histoire Naturelle (H 6)

Formerly the royal botanical gardens, this park contains a small zoo with a hothouse, a maze and some very beautiful old trees. The natural history museum is impressive and houses a number of dinosaur skeletons. The Grande Galerie de l'Evolution has a fascinating display covering all aspects of animal evolution.
Daily (except Tues) 10.00-17.00, Sat/Sun 11.00-18.00; Entrance 40 FF (30 FF before 14.00); Menagerie (small zoo): Daily 09.00-17.00; Entrance 30 FF, children 13 FF; Entrances at Quai Saint-Bernard or Rue Cuvier (5th arr.). Métro: Gare d'Austerlitz, Jussieu

Jardin des Tuileries (E 3)

These formal gardens, lined with dark chestnut trees, run parallel to the Seine between the Louvre and

the Place de la Concorde. They were laid out by Louis XIV's gardener, André Le Nôtre. The Tuileries palace, where Marie-Antoinette spent the last weeks of her freedom, was burnt down by the Commune in 1871. All that remains of it are the Jeu de Paume (tennis court) and the Orangerie (see page 43). The view from the central avenue of the Obelisk in the Place de la Concorde and the Arc de Triomphe beyond is impressive. There are ponies, puppets and a carousel to keep the children entertained.
Avenue du Général-Lemonnier (1st arr.); Métro: Tuileries, Concorde

Parc André Citroën   (O)
This new public park opened in 1992 was laid out on the site of the former Citroën factory. The geometric design and themed flower gardens are fascinating.
Daily 09.00-18.00; Métro: Balard; (15th arr.)

Parc des Buttes-Chaumont   (O)
❧ Designed by Baron Hauss-mann during Napoleon III's reign (1864-67), this hilltop park in the north-east is one of the city's hidden treasures. Streams trickle through it, and there is a waterfall and a 50-m high island in the middle of a lake, which is reached via a footbridge. On the island itself stands a columned temple. The park is a favourite spot with the people from the local districts and you won't find many tourists here. It is one of the few parks in Paris where you are permitted to lie on the grass in fine weather.
Métro: Buttes Chaumont, Botzaris (19th arr.)

Parc Monceau   (C-D 1)
A lush green English-style park in the chic 8th *arrondissement*. It was originally filled with follies: false ruins, Chinese pagodas, temples, Egyptian pyramids and elegant bridges, many of which now lie in ruins. The Musée Nissim de Camondo (*63, Rue de Monceau*) backs onto the park (see page 43).
Daily (except Mon/Tues) 10.00-12.00 and 14.00-17.00; Entrance to museum: 27 FF; The park closes at dusk; Métro: Monceau (8th arr.)

Parc de la Villette   (O)
An ultra-modern city park with science museum, giant spherical cinema, concert hall and a real submarine, all surrounded by expansive lawns and landscaped gardens cut through by a canal. There is always something going on here. A good place to bring the children (see page 40).
Métro: Porte de Pantin or Porte de la Villette (19th arr.)

ROMAN REMAINS

Les Arènes de Lutèce (G 6)
The remains of a Roman arena in the Latin Quarter have been restored in the form of a Gallo-Roman amphitheatre. Old men play *boules* here and the neighbourhood children look upon it as their adventure playground. Open-air concerts and plays are performed here occasionally. Entrances in the Rue de Navarre and the Rue des Arènes.
Métro: Place Monge, Jussieu (5th arr.)

SQUARES

Place de la Concorde (D-E 3)
Laid out during the reign of Louis XV, this magnificent square in the heart of Paris has been the stage for many historical events. Louis XVI, Marie-Antoinette, Danton, and over a thousand others all met their death under the guillotine here. The 27-m high obelisk from Luxor was erected in the 19th century, along with the eight large statues at the edge of the square which represent important French towns such as Lille, Marseille, Brest and Bordeaux.
Métro: Concorde (8th arr.)

Place du Trocadéro (B 3)
⚑ This large square faces the grand neo-classical Palais de Chaillot which houses museums, a cinema and theatre, and the Trocadéro gardens. You get a great view of the Eiffel Tower from here.
Métro: Trocadéro (8th arr.)

Place Vendôme (E 3)
This elegant, formal square dates from the reign of Louis XIV, whose statue once stood in the middle of it. It was torn down during the Revolution to be replaced by the 44-m high Vendôme column erected by Napoleon in celebration of his victories on the battlefield. The Ministry of Justice, the luxury Ritz Hotel and a number of fine jewellers are located here.
Métro: Tuileries (1st arr.)

Place des Victoires (F 3)
Also built to glorify the exploits of the Sun King, this square was given a new lease of life with the arrival of a number of famous fashion designers such as Kenzo, and has since become one of the most exclusive addresses in Paris.
Métro: Bourse (1st arr.)

Place des Vosges (H 4)
★ ☉ Laid out during the reign of Henri IV between 1605 and 1612, this is the oldest square in Paris. The 17th century houses which surround it have been beautifully restored. The park with its fountains is a lovely place to relax in; look out for the back entrance to the Hôtel Sully under the arcades – one of Paris' hidden treasures.
Métro: Chemin Vert, Bastille, St Paul (4th arr.)

THEME PARK

Euro Disneyland (O)
You'll need at least a day to cover the vast resort with its five theme parks. Some spectacular rides.
April-Sept: daily 09.00-23.00, Oct-Mar: Mon-Fri 10.00-18.00, Sat/Sun 09.00-20.00; Entrance: children under 3 no charge, under 11s 130-150 FF, adults 160-195 FF (depending on time of year); Tel: 01 64 74 30 00; 32 km east of Paris; A4 motorway Paris-Nancy; RER, Line A Marne-La-Vallée, 35 FF

Cultural riches

*A wealth of treasures from the old favourites
to new discoveries*

Every year millions of visitors flock to Paris just to visit the museums. The queues for the 'big two', the Louvre and the Musée d'Orsay, are growing ever longer; the revamped Louvre, with its new glass pyramid entrance and added exhibition space, attracts an astonishing six million visitors each year. It is worth taking advantage of the extended opening hours (Mondays and Wednesdays at the Louvre, and Thursdays at the Musée d'Orsay), when the museums stay open until 21.45 and tend to be less crowded.

But it's not just the biggest and best-known museums that are attracting so many people. The smaller and more specialized ones are also becoming increasingly popular. Some have so many treasures, they don't have the space to display more than a fraction of their collection at any one time. Many are set in beautiful grounds or back onto parks where you can enjoy a peaceful rest after your visit and forget for

*The striking glass pyramid entrance
to the Louvre, designed by IM Pei*

a while that you're in the middle of a major metropolis. The choice is inexhaustible and it would take a lot longer than a holiday to do all of the museums in Paris justice. The main thing to remember when planning your itinerary is not to attempt to see too much. It is always difficult to decide how to divide your precious time, but it pays to be selective.

Most state-run museums are closed on Tuesdays and public holidays. The city-run ones usually close on Mondays. The entrance fees average between 20 and 30 FF, and there are concessionary rates for schoolchildren, students and senior citizens. If you intend to visit a number of museums during your stay, then it's definitely worth investing in a *Carte Musées et Monuments*. This pass gives you immediate access to the most popular museums and public monuments, including Versailles, so that you not only save money but also avoid the long queues to get in. The pass costs 80 FF for one day, 160 FF for three days and 240 FF for five consecutive days. It is valid for 65 museums and can be bought at

MARCO POLO SELECTION: MUSEUMS

1 Le Louvre
Mona Lisa is upstaged by the Pyramid (page 41)

2 Musée d'Orsay
Impressionist masterpieces in a former Belle-Epoque railway station (page 44)

3 Musée de la Musique
Part of the vast Cité de la Musique complex (page 40)

4 Musée National du Moyen Age
The 'Lady and the Unicorn' tapestries are the star attraction of this charming medieval museum (page 40)

5 Maison de Victor Hugo
Visit the home of the *The Hunchback of Notre-Dame's* creator (page 42)

6 Musée National Auguste Rodin
Beautiful sculptures set among the roses (page 45)

7 Musée Carnavalet
Crammed with Parisian memorabilia (page 39)

8 La Cité des Sciences et de l'Industrie de la Villette
Ultra-modern science museum and gigantic spherical cinema (page 40)

9 Musée Picasso
The most comprehensive collection of Picasso's work (page 44)

10 Musée de l'Orangerie
Home of Monet's water lilies (page 43)

any one of them. It is also available from the larger métro stations and tourist offices.

The following is just a selection of the hundred or so museums in and around Paris. They are listed in alphabetical order according to the key word rather than the first word, eg Musée de l'*Armée*, Musée d'*Art Moderne*, Musée National d'*Histoire Naturelle*.

Musée de l'Armée – Military Museum (D 4)

Most visitors to the Hôtel des Invalides head straight for the Dôme to see Napoleon's tomb (see page 21). Anyone with an interest in history should also consider visiting the war museum which covers French military history from early times to World War II. Among the exhibits in its collection are battle-scarred armour, Napoleon's own weapons and some of his personal effects, General Daumesnil's wooden leg, and a huge suit of armour which once belonged to an obese count from the Palatinate. If you don't find all this military hardware particularly interesting, then the Musée des Plans-Reliefs on the 4th floor of the Hôtel des Invalides is worth a visit. There are 43 scale models of fortified towns from the 17th to the 19th centuries, which were used by commanders in planning their battle campaigns.

Musée de l'Armée: daily 10.00-17.00; Musée des Plans-Reliefs: daily (except Tues) 10.00-12.00 and 14.00-17.00; Entrance 35 FF; Hôtel des Invalides, 6, Place Vauban (7th arr.); Métro: Varenne, Latour Maubourg, Invalides

Musée d'Art Moderne de la Ville de Paris (C 3)

This modern art museum is housed in the east wing of the Palais de Tokyo. Most of the important 20th-century trends are represented, though the collection is particularly strong on the Fauves, Cubists and the Ecole de Paris. Among the highlights are works by Utrillo, Dufy, Braque, Modigliani, Derain and Matisse, together with frescos by Sonia and Robert Delaunay. Contemporary art exhibitions are also held here on a regular basis.

Daily (except Mon) 10.00-18.00, Wed until 20.30; Entrance to museum: 27 FF; temporary exhibition: 22 FF; 11, Avenue du Président Wilson (16th arr.); Métro: Alma Marceau, Iéna

Musée des Arts Africains et Océaniens (O)

This museum near the Parc de Vincennes is housed in a building originally designed for the great Colonial Exhibition of 1931. The rich collection of tribal art is made up of masks, weapons, jewellery, sculptures and cultural artefacts from the former French colonies in North and Central Africa and the South Pacific. There is an enormous aquarium in the basement which contains tropical fish, giant turtles and even crocodiles.

Daily (except Tues) 10.00-12.00 and 13.30-17.20; Entrance 30FF; 293, Avenue Daumesnil (12th arr.); Métro: Porte Dorée

Musée Carnavalet (H 4)

★ This fascinating museum of Parisian history in the Marais is worth visiting just to see the beautiful Renaissance mansions it occupies. It was originally housed in the Hôtel Carnavalet where Mme de Sévigné lived in the 17th century, but was later extended into the neighbouring Hôtel Le Pelletier. The displays of paintings, maps, topographical models and photographs illustrate just how dramatic and turbulent the history of Paris has been; the brutality of some of the changes that occurred during the evolution of the city and its many stages of development are vividly portrayed. One of the most interesting exhibits is the model of the Ile de la Cité in the Middle Ages which shows just how densely built up the area around Notre-Dame was before it was cleared in the 19th century. When Baron Haussmann redesigned vast areas of Paris during the Second Empire in the 1850s and 60s, many of the old buildings were razed to the ground to make way for the grand avenues. Thankfully, some architectural elements, interior features and contents escaped destruction and found their way to the Carnavalet.

The museum has a particularly rich collection of documents and miscellaneous items from the Revolution – a model of the Bastille built from the original stone, little guillotines made of bone, a lock of Robespierre's hair and his last letter, spattered with blood, as well as everyday objects decorated with Revolutionary symbols. There is also a fascinating array of objects salvaged from the Napoleonic period, including luggage, socks and cutlery used by the Emperor on campaign and when he was in exile.

Daily (except Mon) 10.00-17.40; Entrance 35 FF; 23, Rue de Sévigné (3rd arr.); Métro: St Paul, Chemin Vert

Musée du Cinéma – Film Museum (B 3)

Henri Langlois, film fanatic and founder of the Paris Cinémathèque, was an avid collector of films and memorabilia. His vast collection covers 80 years of cinema history. Posters and stills, sets and backdrops, magic lanterns, costumes, a suit worn by Charlie Chaplin, a dress worn by Ingrid Bergman, one of Buster Keaton's hats – these are but of few of the hundreds of fascinating objects imaginatively displayed here. A guided tour of the museum lasts about two hours. The Cinémathèque du Chaillot, next door, screens old films daily.

Tours daily (except Mon/Tues) at 10, 11, 14, 15, 16 and 17.00; Entrance 30 FF; Palais de Chaillot, Place du Trocadéro (16th arr.); Métro: Trocadéro

Cité de la Musique – Music Museum (O)

★ The music museum in the ultra-modern Cité de la Musique features a collection of 4500 musical instruments from the 16th century to the present day. You can also amuse yourself with interactive electronic sound displays. The music complex is part of the vast Parc de la Villette development (see below) and includes a library and a concert hall.

Daily (except Mon) 12.00-18.00, until 21.30 on Fri, 10.00-18.00 on Sun; Entrance 35 FF; 221, Av. Jean Jaurès (19th arr.); Métro: Porte de Pantin

La Cité des Sciences et de l'Industrie – Museum of Science, Technology and Industry (O)

★ ⚹ From a distance, this incredible construction on the outskirts of north-eastern Paris looks like a space station. The Pompidou Centre is small by comparison. There is so much to see and do here. The interactive displays are both fun and educational, teaching you about aspects of modern technology, space, ecology, climate, energy etc.

Just in front of the science museum is La Géode, a gigantic spherical cinema. Films on nature and space travel are projected onto its 1000 sq m circular screen. It's best to buy tickets for the Géode at the entrance to the complex, or to order them in advance (avoid Wednesdays if you can as most available spaces are booked up by school parties).

Daily (except Mon) 10.00-18.00, until 21.30 on Fri; Entrance fees: Cité des Sciences 50 FF; Music Museum 35 FF, La Géode 57 FF; 30, Rue Corentin Cariou (19th arr.); Métro: Porte de la Villette, Porte de Pantin

Musée de Cluny – Museum of the Middle Ages (F 5)

★ Housed in a medieval mansion, by the remains of the 3rd-century Roman baths in the heart of the Latin Quarter, this unique museum displays artefacts, furniture, jewellery and weapons from the Middle Ages, as well as ancient sculptures. Two of the most fascinating exhibits are the recently unearthed stone heads of the kings of Judea from Notre-Dame, and a series of six remarkable tapestries known as the *Lady with the Unicorn* which depict a lady flanked by a unicorn and a lion. The detail is simply breathtaking and it is worth visiting the often uncrowded museum to see this work of art alone.

Daily (except Tues) 09.15-17.45; 6, Place Paul Painlevé (5th arr.); Métro: Cluny-La Sorbonne, St Michel, Odéon

Musée Delacroix (F 4)

The house where artist Eugène Delacroix lived and painted is tucked away in a quiet, pretty square in St-Germain-des-Prés. It has been renovated and converted into a museum which looks out onto a charming garden. The collection is made up of paintings, drawings and manuscripts by the Romantic master.

Daily (except Tues) 10.00-17.00; Entrance 22 FF; 6, Rue de Furstemberg (6th arr.); Métro: Mabillon, St-Germain-des-Prés

Musée Grévin – Waxworks (F 2)

Historic scenes and famous French people are represented here – the Royal Family in prison during the Revolution, Joan of Arc on her way to the stake, Marat murdered in his bath (the bath is actually the original), alongside leading contemporary figures including Mitterand and Jean-Paul Belmondo. There is a hall of mirrors which is popular with children. Expensive fun.

Daily 13.00-19.00 (during Parisian holidays from 10.00-19.00); Entrance 55 FF; 10, Boulevard Montmartre; Métro: Rue Montmartre

Musée National d'Histoire Naturelle (H 6)

The Natural History Museum in the Jardin des Plantes has a fascinating collection of prehistoric skeletons, minerals and insects. The highlight of the museum is the Grande Galerie de l'Evolution, where the history of evolution is illustrated with the help of light and sound effects (see p. 33).

Daily (except Tues) 10.00-18.00, Thurs until 22.00; Entrance 40 FF; 57, Rue Cuvier (5th arr.); Métro: Monge, Jussieu

Musée de l'Homme (B 3)

In the west wing of the Palais de Chaillot, this museum traces the history of mankind through anthropological and ethnological displays: artefacts, sculptures, jewellery, clothing, and weaponry from all five continents.

Daily (except Tues) 10.00-17.00; Entrance 30 FF; Place du Trocadéro; Métro: Trocadéro

Musée du Louvre (F 3-4)

★ ⚹ The Louvre Palace was turned into a museum just after the Revolution in 1793. Originally a fortress built in the 12th century by King Philippe Auguste, it was gradually extended over four centuries into a magnificent royal residence – structural improvements are still being made today. The Cour Carrée at the eastern end dates from Louis XIV's reign and is a fine example of Renaissance architecture. The splendid façade facing the Seine is part Renaissance, part Napoleonic. At the western end of the main courtyard is the Arc du Carrousel, a small Arc de Triomphe built to commemorate Napoleon's victories. But the Cour Napoléon is now dominated by the glass pyramid which has become one of the city's major attractions. Designed by the Chinese-American architect Ieoh Ming Pei and opened in 1989, the pyramid is surrounded by a magnificent square, and provides a fascinating contrast with the old building. During construction of the pyramid and the entrance hall beneath it, the foundation walls of the medieval fortress were excavated and have been left exposed. After extensive building work, the Richelieu wing, which formerly housed the

Ministry of Finance, was connected directly to the museum, finally bringing the 'Grand Louvre' into being. Exhibition space has been almost doubled, resulting at last in a modern visitor-friendly museum. With the new wing, the Louvre is attracting record numbers and more than six million people now visit the museum annually. Admittedly there is often a queue to get in, but it's worth the wait.

From the entrance hall, you have access to all seven sections of the museum: 1. Oriental Antiquities 2. Egyptian Antiquities 3. Greek and Roman Antiquities 4. Paintings (with 10 sub-sections: Old French painting; Old Dutch painting; Old German painting; 16th century French painting; 17th century French painting; Italian painting up to the 17th century; Spanish painting; Flemish painting; 18th century French painting; 19th century French painting) 5. Sculpture from the Middle Ages to the Present Day 6. Furniture and Crafts 7. Etchings and Drawings.

Millions of people come from all over the world to see the three most famous works in the museum, the *Venus de Milo,* the *Nike of Samothrace* and, of course, the *Mona Lisa* (also known as *La Gioconda*), which is secured behind bullet-proof glass and not easy to get a good view of. Of the other Leonardos, the *Madonna of the Grotto* should certainly be sought out. The Egyptian department is quite remarkable and well worth taking time over.

Apart from one of the world's greatest collections of art, the Louvre offers visitors numerous other attractions. You can attend lectures, go to concerts and films, browse in Europe's largest art bookshop and visit the new Carrousel du Louvre shopping arcade, with its 29 boutiques and 15 restaurants.

Daily (except Tues) 09.00-18.00, Mon and Wed until 21.45, pyramid until 22.00; Entrance 45 FF until 15.00, 26 FF from 15.00 and all day Sun; under 18s free. 1st Sunday of the month is free. You are free to leave the museum and return on the same day; Métro: Palais Royal, Musée du Louvre, Tuileries (1st arr.)

Maison de Balzac   (A 4)
Honoré de Balzac lived in this house in the 16th *arrondissement* from 1840 until 1847. At the time the area was still quite rural, and the house with its little garden retains much of its original charm. It was here that the prolific novelist penned much of the monumental *Comédie Humaine.* The museum provides an insight into his life and work through an interesting and varied collection that includes original manuscripts, portraits of himself and his beloved Eva Hanska, letters, a large library, his desk and various other personal belongings. Balzac reputedly wrote for 16 hours a day, keeping himself awake with copious amounts of coffee at night. The famous coffee pot in which the brew was made is also on display.

Daily (except Mon) 10.00-17.40; 47, Rue Raynouard (16th arr.); Métro: Passy, La Muette

Maison de Victor Hugo   (H 4)
★ The great 19th-century poet and novelist Victor Hugo lived in this 17th-century town house on the magnificent Place des Vosges

The Carrousel du Louvre

The fantastic new underground shopping complex known as the Carrousel du Louvre stretches from the entrance hall under the pyramid to the inverted pyramid at the western end of the Cour Napoléon. Boutiques, cafés, fast-food outlets, even a Virgin Megastore complete with listening posts and books, can all be found here. Opening times are the same as the museums which means you can shop here on a Sunday too. The Carrousel also houses concert halls and conference rooms, and now hosts most of the top international fashion shows. As you might expect, the boutiques are not exactly cheap, but it's fun to window-shop.

from 1832 until the revolution of 1848. His former apartments are now filled with drawings, manuscripts, letters and other objects relating to his life and work. It was here that he wrote *Les Misérables*. The view over the Place des Vosges is splendid.
Daily (except Mon) 10.00-17.40; Entrance 27 FF; 6, Place des Vosges (4th arr.); Métro: Bastille, St Paul, Chemin Vert

Musée Marmottan (O)
The wealthy art historian Paul Marmottan put an amazing collection together and established this foundation, which he bequeathed along with his mansion to the city. Look out for the medieval miniatures and the Impressionist paintings in the left wing of the building. The famous masterpiece by Monet, *Impression Soleil Levant*, from which the movement took its name, is here together with a number of the artist's garden and water lily scenes. There are, in all, around 150 works by Monet on view, along with paintings by Renoir, Sisley, Pissarro and Signac.
Daily (except Mon) 10.00-17.30; Entrance 40 FF; 2, Rue Louis-Boilly (16th arr.); Métro: La Muette

Musée des Arts de la Mode et du Textile (F 3)
The Museum of Fashion in the Louvre boasts a rich collection of costumes, shoes, accessories, sketches and documents illustrating the evolution of haute couture in the fashion capital. Temporary exhibitions are held every six months.
Daily (except Mon) 11.00-18.00, until 22.00 on Wed; Entrance 25 FF; Palais du Louvre, 107, Rue de Rivoli (1st arr.); Métro: Palais-Royal, Musée du Louvre

Musée Nissim de Camondo (D 1)
Housed in a splendid building on the outskirts of Parc Monceau, this museum is filled with treasure collected by a rich Jewish banking family. Count Camondo commissioned the building in 1914 to house the family collection which includes 18th-century furniture and paintings among other precious objects.
Daily (except Mon and Tues) 10.00-17.00; Entrance 27 FF; 63, Rue Monceau (8th arr.); Métro: Villiers

Musée de l'Orangerie (E 3)
★ Spend an unforgettable hour or so in the Orangerie in the company of Cézanne, Renoir,

Rousseau, Matisse, Picasso, Derain, and the eight large water lily paintings which Monet painted in his garden at Giverny.

Daily (except Tues) 09.45-17.15; Entrance 27 FF; the water lily rooms are sometimes closed at lunch time; Place de la Concorde (1st arr.); Métro: Concorde

Musée d'Orsay (E 4)

★ ⟲ This museum has been one of the most popular ever since it opened in 1986. Paris needed a museum for 19th-century art to fill the gap left between the Musée du Louvre and the Pompidou Centre. What better place for it than the disused Belle Epoque railway station (which was very nearly demolished in 1970). It was originally built for the 1900 World Fair, but was not used for very long as the platforms proved to be too short. The museum occupies the old station hall, which was converted by the Italian architect Gae Aulenti who kept as many of its original features as possible, covering it with a glass roof.

The salon painters of the Second Empire are well represented here and the central aisle is full of beautiful sculptures, but the biggest attraction is the Impressionist gallery which features works by all the masters of the movement – Manet, Pissarro, Monet, Renoir, Sisley, Rousseau, Van Gogh, Toulouse-Lautrec, Gauguin, and Cézanne. Among the museum's greatest masterpieces are: *Le Déjeuner sur l'Herbe, Olympia* and *Le Balcon* by Manet; *Moulin de la Galette* and *Déjeuner des Canotiers* by Renoir; and *La Chambre Jaune* by Van Gogh. Apart from the main exhibition

there are some remarkable displays of furniture, photographs, art nouveau design and cinematography. A fine view of the Louvre and Sacré-Coeur can be seen from the restaurant and upper galleries – don't let the long queues put you off.

Daily (except Mon) 10.00-18.00, Sun 09.00-18.00, Thurs 10.00-21.45; Entrance 36 FF; under 18s free; 1, Rue de Bellechasse (7th arr.); Métro: Solférino

Musée Picasso (H 3)

★ ⟲ The unique collection of Picasso's works, which he himself assembled, was given to the French State in lieu of inheritance tax after the artist's death. There are around 200 of his paintings, as well as sculptures, collages, drawings, and ceramics, all housed in a magnificent 17th-century mansion. The walk to the museum through the Marais is a delightful one.

Daily (except Tues) 09.45-17.15, Wed until 22.00; Entrance 35 FF; under 18s free; Hôtel Salé, 5, Rue de Thorigny (3rd arr.); Métro: St Paul, Filles du Calvaire, St Sébastien Froissart

Pompidou Centre (G 4)

⟲ When the Pompidou Centre was first opened in 1977 it caused something of a stir. It was designed by Richard Rogers and Renzo Piano, who placed the structural elements, usually concealed within, on the outside. Twenty years ago such a high-tech building with its massive coloured pipes, ducts and steel frame came as a shock to the public who had seen nothing like it. Now it is one of the city's most familiar landmarks and, with around 7 million visitors a year,

Musée d'Orsay, the converted station

it is the most visited museum in Paris. The five-storey cultural centre, referred to by Parisians as Beaubourg (the medieval name for the district), is home to the National Museum of Modern Art. Apart from many exhibition rooms, it houses an enormous library, a design centre, a cinema, a centre for experimental music, a bookshop, restaurant and a rooftop cafeteria. A ride on the escalators, set within a transparent tube on the façade, is free. They take you up to the 5th floor where there's a sweeping view across the rooftops of Paris, from Notre-Dame to the Sacré-Coeur.

The Museum of Modern Art is on the 4th floor. All the major movements of the 20th century are represented here, from Fauvism, Cubism, Abstraction, Surrealism and Dadaism through the most important post-war trends, Pop Art, New Realism, right up to the present day. The collection includes works by all the 20th century masters – Matisse, Picasso, Braque, Kandinsky, Max Ernst, Henry Moore etc. – and

the museum is constantly acquiring new works. The Grande Galerie on the 5th floor is reserved for temporary exhibitions. These are highly publicized beforehand and usually generate a great deal of excitement, attracting hundreds of thousands of visitors.

Beaubourg's popularity has taken its toll, however, and unfortunately it is currently closed for desperately needed refurbishment and enlargement. The festive reopening is due to take place on New Year's Eve 1999 when the millennium clock outside completes its countdown to the end of the century. Certain parts of the building are still open to the public, and you can visit the beautiful Brancusi studio nearby (*daily, except Tues, 10.00-22.00; Entrance 20 FF*). Information on exhibitions and events in and around the centre can be obtained from the tent in the forecourt (*daily, except Tues*).
Place Beaubourg (4th arr.); Métro: Rambuteau, Les Halles, Hôtel de Ville

Musée Rodin (D 4)

★ The Hôtel Biron, where Auguste Rodin, the most important French sculptor of the late 19th century, lived and worked, lies in an oasis of peace and greenery between the Hôtel des Invalides and the government ministries. Here you can see the artist's best-known works, including *The Kiss*, *The Thinker*, *The Burghers of Calais*, *Balzac* and *Danaïde*. The garden has been planted with a fantastic array of roses – an added bonus in fine weather.
Daily (except Mon) 10.00-17.00; Entrance 32 FF (garden 5 FF); Hôtel Biron, 77, Rue de Varenne (7th arr.); Métro: Varenne

Where to eat

*Heavenly cuisine for well-padded wallets
and shoestring budgets*

Restaurants of every size and description abound in Paris, ranging from gastronomic temples to small bistros, brasseries and cafés. Anyone interested in investigating French regional cookery will be able to find a restaurant specializing in local dishes from anywhere in France. You can sample Normandy's unique combinations of cream, pork and apples, with cider or calvados; fish stews like *bouillabaisse* and *bourride,* and characteristic herb-scented dishes from Provence; rustic dishes of the Auvergne; from the southwest, *foie gras* made from specially fattened duck and goose livers, and *cassoulet* – a casserole of beans enriched with various meats and sausage. Brasseries serving *sauerkraut* and pork specialities from Alsace are dotted all over Paris, while Montparnasse still has the largest concentration of Breton *crêperies* serving savoury and sweet pancakes traditionally washed down with cider.

A café terrace, an art nouveau bistro or a gourmet palace – when it comes to food, you're spoiled for choice

In recent years, many leading chefs have moved away from the rich food and heavy sauces of classic traditional French cooking, and are concentrating on innovative, lighter dishes composed of fresh but unexpected ingredients and flavours. The nouvelle cuisine trend that took root in the 1980s is still prevalent in many places. When carefully thought out and well prepared, nouvelle cuisine can be very satisfying, but it can be equally disappointing, resulting all too often in unhappy combinations served in small portions at great expense. Many of the more serious-minded chefs and restaurateurs, however, while still inventing new dishes, have realized once again the virtues of some of the lighter traditional dishes, and are combining these and nouvelle cuisine on their menus.

Ethnic restaurants, once few and far between, have proliferated in recent years. You can now find Chinese and Vietnamese restaurants everywhere and it is worth looking out for specialists in Italian, Japanese, Lebanese, Moroccan, Algerian, Russian and South American cooking.

Paris has countless specialist food shops that sell delicious take-away snacks. You'll come across a wide variety of delicatessens (*charcuteries, épiceries fines, traiteurs*), bakeries (*boulangeries*) and cake shops (*pâtisseries*). For a sit-down snack or just something to drink there are plenty of options, with cafés, snack bars, *crêperies, bars-à-vin* and *salons-de-thé* around every corner. A classic café menu will offer, among other things, a *croque monsieur* (cheese and ham toasted sandwich) or *croque madame* (the same with an egg on top), a *salade niçoise*, or good old steak and chips. The *salons-de-thé* have an excellent choice of fine teas served with irresistible cakes and pastries. The *bars-à-vin* offer wine by the glass or bottle, selected by the *patron*, which you can accompany with a side dish of ham, cheese or other appetizer.

For a more substantial meal, there is an endless choice of bistros, brasseries and restaurants in every price range. Like many aspects of modern French life, the rise of the restaurant has its roots in the Revolution. Cooks and kitchen staff who had been employed by the aristocracy soon found themselves out of work and opened small establishments, inviting the bourgeoisie to eat like the nobility. Balzac and Zola described this phenomenon and Daumier drew it.

The bistro is where it all began. Originally a simple, unpretentious restaurant, a true bistro has a tiled floor, a large bar, mirrors on the wall, and checked tablecloths, and offers moderately-priced but wholesome food. The menu with its dish of the day is usually posted outside or chalked up on a blackboard. Bistros have become increasingly fashionable

MARCO POLO SELECTION: RESTAURANTS

1 Polidor
Good old-fashioned cuisine in the Latin Quarter (page 57)

2 Julien
Friendly and fashionable art nouveau brasserie (page 51)

3 Café Marly
The Louvre's stylish café overlooks the pyramid (page 55)

4 A la Tour de Montlhéry – Chez Denise
Down-to-earth bistro in Les Halles district (page 53)

5 Bofinger
The oldest brasserie in Paris (page 51)

6 L'Ambroisie
Exquisite food in the lovely Place des Vosges (page 54)

7 Moissonnier
Friendly bistro with Burgundian slant (page 52)

8 Le Train Bleu
Grand station restaurant with magnificent belle époque décor (page 55)

9 L'Echanson
Wine bar with excellent cuisine (page 52)

10 Beauvilliers
Wickedly priced, but a unique experience in Montmartre (page 54)

and many are now so refined that they have overtaken the best restaurants in the quality of their food. Remember, the prices reflect this trend and in some of the top bistros you have to book a table days in advance.

A brasserie falls somewhere between a simple bistro and a restaurant. A typical brasserie is big and noisy, with long opening hours and an extensive menu featuring traditional Alsatian dishes such as sauerkraut and sausages, and a wide variety of beers and Alsatian wine.

Breakfast (*petit déjeuner*) is fairly standard throughout France: *café au lait*, a slice of baguette with butter and jam, or a *croissant*, *brioche*, *pain au chocolat* or *pain au raisin*. You can choose to have breakfast in your hotel room, but unless it's included in the price you're better off having it in a nearby café (many Parisians eat theirs standing at the bar).

Lunch (*déjeuner*), while much lighter than it used to be, is still fairly substantial. At around 12.30 office workers pour into the bistros and order a quick menu or the *plat du jour*. A lunchtime menu usually consists of a light *hors d'oeuvre* followed by a meat or fish dish with salad or vegetables, a basket of bread, and maybe a half-carafe of wine. Dessert is usually either a yoghurt or a slice of tart or flan, or cheese, immediately followed by a small, strong black coffee (*express*).

The most important meal of the day is the evening meal. *Le dîner* is usually eaten between 19.00 and 21.00, sometimes later. If you want a bite to eat after the theatre or cinema a number of places serve late supper (*souper*).

The city is scattered with classic bistros and brasseries

A full-blown evening meal begins with an aperitif – most typically a pastis (aniseed-flavoured drink with ice and water) or kir (white wine with blackcurrant liqueur) – followed by a starter (*hors d'oeuvre, entrée*), main dish (meat or fish with vegetables), then cheese and/or dessert. When ordering your meat you will be expected to specify how you want it cooked. Waiters don't always ask and will usually serve it on the rare side unless you request it otherwise. There are four types of *cuisson*: *bleu* is almost raw, *saignant* is rare, *à point* is medium and *bien cuit* is well done. The French generally prefer their meat *saignant*. As accompaniment to meat and cheese the usual choice is red wine, and for fish and poultry it's generally a dry white.

You always get plenty of bread with your meal – usually white, but sometimes darker varieties (*pain de campagne*) are offered. A carafe of tap water will be brought to your table automatically, but you can also order bottled water if you prefer (sparkling water is *l'eau gazeuse*, and still water is *l'eau naturelle*). Although wine is the preferred drink with a meal you can, of course, order beer, especially in the brasseries.

The main dish is often followed by a salad before the cheese selection is brought to the table. A little cheese, with a glass of good red wine, is an important part of any menu. If you have room for dessert, most waiters reel off a standard choice which might typically include a fruit tart, *tarte tatin* (upside down apple tart), *crème caramel, mousse au chocolat,* ice cream and profiteroles. It is customary to finish off a meal with a strong black *café express.* If you really want to pull out all the stops, you can order an after-dinner drink with your coffee. *Digestifs* on offer usually include Cognac, Calvados or Marc.

Most places accept credit cards these days, but it's best to check beforehand. A service charge is always included in the bill, but it is also customary to add a small tip – no less than 10 FF – and to leave it on the table.

The following list of recommended cafés and restaurants is by no means exhaustive, but should give you some idea of the variety on offer.

CAFES, SALONS DE THES, SNACK BARS & ICE-CREAM PARLOURS

T = Terrace

Angélina (E 3)
Delightful belle époque café, famous for its divine hot chocolate. The cakes and pastries are equally mouth-watering. Well-heeled clientele and prices to match. Expect queues.

Daily 09.30-19.00, closed Aug; 226, Rue de Rivoli (1st arr.); Métro: Tuileries

Café Beaubourg (T) (G 4)
☂ Popular, modern café that looks on to the Pompidou Centre, with interior by Philippe Starck. Stylish clientele. Good brunch and salads, but not cheap.
Daily 10.00-02.00; Rue St-Martin, corner of Place Beaubourg (4th arr.); Métro: Hôtel de Ville

Berthillon (H 5)
The most famous ice cream parlour in Paris, Berthillon is an institution. There are dozens of different flavoured ice creams and sorbets on offer. Don't let the rather uninspiring shop exterior put you off. Expect long queues in hot weather.
Daily (except Mon/Tues) 10.00-20.00, closed July and Aug; 31, Rue St-Louis-en-Ile (4th arr.); Métro: Pont Marie

Les Deux Magots (T) (F 4)
The most famous of Parisian cafés and arguably the most attractive. Formerly a meeting place for intellectuals and literary giants such as Breton, Sartre and Simone de Beauvoir, today it is overrun with tourists. The hot chocolate, reputed to be the best in Paris, is expensive and overrated. However, in the morning sun, there's still a certain magic about this legendary café.
Daily 08.00-02.00, closed Aug; 170, Boulevard St-Germain (6th arr.); Métro: St-Germain-des-Prés

Café de Flore (T) (F 4)
Next to Les Deux Magots this café, once patronized by Camus and Sartre, is still popular with the intelligentsia, as well as rich

teenagers and tourists. The terrace is nice enough, but it's more atmospheric inside. Street entertainers ply their trade here during the summer months.
Daily 08.00-02.00, closed July; 172, Boulevard St-Germain (6th arr.); Métro: St-Germain-des-Prés

Café de la Paix (T)   (E 2)
Despite the number of tourists that flock here, this 19th-century café with its splendid décor is still full of charm. A great place to sit and watch the activity around the Opéra, day and night.
Daily 09.00-02.00; Place de l'Opéra (9th arr.); Métro: Opéra

BISTROS, BRASSERIES & BARS-A-VIN

Category 1
(From around 300 FF per person, including wine)

Chez Benoît (T)   (G 4)
Exceptionally beautiful and luxurious belle époque surroundings, everything here is just as it should be: reception, menu, price, atmosphere. Book well in advance. No credit cards.
Closed Sat/Sun and Aug; 20, Rue St-Martin (4th arr.); Tel. 01 42 72 25 76; Métro: Châtelet, Hôtel de Ville

Bofinger (T)   (H 4)
★ Said to be the oldest brasserie in Paris, the legendary Bofinger is certainly one of the most attractive. The large dining area is illuminated by a vast glass dome. Oysters are a speciality and the menu is varied. Just off the Place de la Bastille.
Daily until 01.00; 3-7, Rue de la Bastille (4th arr.); Tel. 01 42 72 87 82; Métro: Bastille

Julien   (G 2)
★ It's worth coming here just to see the wonderful décor of this fashionable art nouveau brasserie that draws wealthy people to a not-so-wealthy area. Quality food. Advance booking essential.
Daily until 01.30; 16, Rue du Faubourg St-Denis (9th arr.); Tel. 01 47 70 12 06; Métro: Strasbourg St-Denis

Brasserie Lipp   (F 4)
Famous throughout the world, this St-Germain-des-Prés establishment is a favourite among politicians and artists. Specialities include *choucroute* (sauerkraut with pork) and pickled herrings. No advance booking.
Daily (except Mon) 12.00-01.00, closed July; 151, Boulevard St-Germain (6th arr.); Métro: St-Germain-des-Prés

Category 2
(From around 200 FF per person, including wine)

Chez André (T)   (C 2)
Typical bistro décor and traditional bistro fare in the Champs-Elysées area. Menu handwritten by the chef. Dish of the day both at midday and in the evening.
Daily until 01.00; 12, Rue Marbeuf (8th arr.); Tel. 01 47 20 59 57; Métro: Franklin-D. Roosevelt

Balzar (T)   (F 5)
Brasserie and café in the Latin Quarter, by the Sorbonne. Classic brasserie décor – mirrors, copper, and plants. *Choucroute* (sauerkraut and sausage) and beer are staple fare, and the menu offers an interesting variety of fish dishes.
Daily 10.00-00.30, closed Aug; 49, Rue des Ecoles (5th arr.); Tel. 01 43 54 13 67; Métro: St Michel

Le Boeuf-sur-le-Toit (T)   **(C 2)**
Beautifully restored, large, elegant brasserie in the Champs-Elysées district. Impressive choice of oysters and shellfish. Always busy, so book in advance.
Daily until 02.00; 34, Rue du Colisée (8th arr.); Tel. 01 43 59 83 81; Métro: Franklin-D. Roosevelt

Aux Charpentiers (T)   **(F 5)**
Unpretentious bistro in the St-Germain area, well-known for its reasonably priced specialities like brawn in vinaigrette, or hare in mustard sauce. Popular with the Left Bank intelligentsia.
Daily (except Sun); 10, Rue Mabillon (6th arr.); Tel. 01 43 26 30 05; Métro: Mabillon

La Coupole   **(E 6)**
❂ A Parisian institution, this Montparnasse brasserie is the largest in the city. It boasts an amazing art deco interior and offers a good choice of oysters, shellfish, veal and sauerkraut. Stylish and always fashionable. Book in advance.
Daily until 02.00; 102, Boulevard du Montparnasse (14th arr.); Tel. 01 43 20 14 20; Métro: Vavin

L'Echanson   **(O)**
★ Wine bar/bistro with excellent cuisine. Popular with both locals and prominent figures who come here to escape the limelight.
Daily (except Sun and Mon lunchtime), 89, Rue Daguerre (14th arr.); Tel. 01 43 22 20 00; Métro: Gaité

Epi d'Or   **(F 3)**
Old-fashioned bistro near Les Halles, famed for its ox-tongue salad, hot apple pies and good wine. Especially popular among the film and media crowd.
Daily (except Sat pm/Sun), closed Aug; 25, Rue Jean-Jacques-Rousseau (1st arr.); Tel. 01 42 36 38 12; Métro: Palais Royal

Brasserie Flo   **(G 2)**
The location in an arcade off the Rue St-Denis may not be immediately appealing, but this atmospheric brasserie is always full. Lovely, dark interior décor from the 1900s. Fish and pork are among the specialities.
Open daily; 7, Cour des Petites-Ecuries (10th arr.); Tel. 01 47 70 13 59; Métro: Château d'Eau

Brasserie de l'Ile St-Louis (T) (G 5)
Lovely old and very lively brasserie, with good, traditional menu. Popular with British and American expats.
Daily until 01.30 (except Wed/Thurs pm), closed Aug; 55, Quai de Bourbon (4th arr.); Tel. 01 43 54 02 59; Métro: Pont Marie

Moissonnier   **(G 5)**
★ ⚘ Tasty Lyonnaise specialities are offered at reasonable prices and there is an appetizing help-yourself hors d'oeuvre bar with plenty of choice. Cosy atmosphere and a friendly clientele. Always busy.
Daily (except Sun evening, Mon), closed Aug; 28, Rue des Fossés-St-Bernard (5th arr.); Tel. 01 43 29 87 65; Métro: Cardinal Lemoine

Square Trousseau (T)   **(I 5)**
Long-established and unpretentious bistro on a pretty tree-lined square. Outside seating in summer. Not far from the lively Marché d'Aligre. A hidden gem.
Daily (except Sun/Mon); 1, Rue Antoine-Vollon (12th arr.); Tel. 01 43 43 06 00; Métro: Ledru Rollin

A la Tour de Montlhéry – Chez Denise (F 3)

★ A model bistro, with an excellent menu. Everything here is just as it should be: the service, the food and the atmosphere.

Open 24 hrs (except Sat/Sun), closed 14 July to 15 Aug; 5, Rue des Prouvaires (1st arr.); Tel. 01 42 36 21 82; Métro: Louvre, Châtelet-Les Halles

Brasserie le Vaudeville (T) (F 2)

Spacious art deco brasserie near the stock exchange (*La Bourse*). A popular lunchtime spot with financiers and journalists, always busy and lively. Good fish and shellfish, and a wide selection of desserts.

Daily; 29, Rue Vivienne (2nd arr.); Tel. 01 42 33 39 31; Métro: Bourse

---

The Gourmet Palaces of Paris

Le Grand Véfour (F 3)

Vast restaurant with beautiful 18th century décor in the Palais Royal. From 600 FF per head.

Daily (except Sat/Sun (closed Aug); 17, Rue de Beaujolais (1st arr.); Tel. 01 42 96 56 27; Métro: Pyramides

L'Arpège (D 4)

Since Alain Passard was awarded a 3rd Michelin star, his restaurant has shot to fame. The master chef's specialities include lobster in white wine, suckling pig with sage, and aniseed ice cream. From 1000 FF per head.

Daily (except Sat and Sun lunchtime); 84, Rue de Varenne (7th arr.); Tel. 01 45 51 47 33; Métro: Varenne

Jules Verne (B 4)

Delicious food with a panoramic view of Paris. The legendary Eiffel Tower restaurant has its own lift which takes customers up to the second platform. The prices are equally elevated and tables hard to obtain. From 600 FF.

Daily until 23.00; Tour Eiffel; Tel. 01 45 55 20 04; Métro: Bir Hakeim

Tour d'Argent (G 5)

Magnificent view of Notre-Dame. Duck a speciality. 2 Michelin stars. From 700 FF.

Daily (except Mon); 15, Quai de la Tournelle (5th arr.); Tel. 01 43 54 23 31; Métro: Maubert Mutualité

Lucas-Carton (E 2)

Excellent food in belle époque surroundings created by Alain Senderens, 'the most gifted chef in all Paris'. 3 Michelin stars. From 800 FF.

Daily except Sat/Sun (closed on public holidays and in Aug); 9, Place de la Madeleine (8th arr.); Tel. 01 42 65 22 90; Métro: Madeleine

Taillevent (B 2)

One of the most elegant and dignified restaurants in Paris. The menu offers traditional as well as modern fare and the wine list is remarkable. 3 stars in the Michelin guide. There are only a few tables, so you will have to book months in advance. From 500 FF.

Daily except Sat/Sun (closed on public holidays and in Aug); 15, Rue Lamennais (8th arr.); Tel. 01 45 63 39 94; Métro: Etoile

Category 3
(From around 100 FF per person,
including wine)

Bouillon Racine (F 5)
A beautifully restored bistro in the
Latin Quarter, with good Alsatian
cuisine and a range of beers.
*Mon-Sat 11.00-01.00; 3, Rue Racine
(6th arr.); Tel. 01 44 32 15 60; Métro:
Odéon*

Café Charbon (I 2)
Simple but tasty food in the
Belleville area. Good place for
Sunday brunch. Evenings can get
crowded.
*Daily 12.00-02.00, Sun open for
brunch; 109, Rue Oberkampf (11th
arr.); Tel. 01 43 57 55 13; Métro:
Parmentier*

Au Cochon à l'Oreille (G3)
Classic Parisian bistro decorated
with wonderful tiles depicting
scenes of the old market. Authentic atmosphere, where local
butchers and fishmongers sit
comfortably alongside punks and
trendsetters at the bar. Steak,
chips, red wine and Calvados.
Reasonable prices. Behind the
church of St-Eustache.
*Daily (except Sun) 05.30-17.00; 15,
Rue Montmartre (1st arr.); Tel. 01 42
36 07 56; Métro: Etienne Marcel,
Les Halles*

Au Crus de Bourgogne (G 3)
Unpretentious checked table-
cloth bistro in the Sentier district.
Classic menu, but if you fancy
something special you can treat
yourself to fresh lobster mayon-
naise or pâté de foie gras. Very
reasonable. Regular clientele.
*Daily (except Sat/Sun), closed Aug;
3, Rue de Bachaumont (2nd arr.); Tel.
01 42 33 48 24; Métro: Sentier*

Category 1
(From around 400 FF per person,
including wine)

L'Ambroisie (H 4)
★ Excellent restaurant in a re-
stored town house on the Place
des Vosges. Book well in advance.
*Daily (except Sun/Mon pm) 12.00-
14.00 and 20.00-22.30; 9, Place des
Vosges (4th arr.); Tel. 01 42 78 51 41;
Métro: St Paul*

L'Assiette (O)
Lucette Rousseau, more familiarly
known as 'Lulu', conjures up delicious dishes in this charming converted Montparnasse charcuterie.
A popular haunt with journalists
and people in the fashion industry.
Advance booking essential.
*Daily (except Mon/Tues), closed Aug
and Easter; 181, Rue du Château
(14th arr.); Tel. 01 43 22 64 86;
Métro: Mouton Duvernet*

Beauvilliers (O)
★ Second Empire restaurant, high
up in Montmartre. Flowers, silver
and porcelain add to the festive atmosphere. Fine French cuisine for
an international clientele. The
covered terrace offers a wonderful
view. Advance booking essential.
*Daily (except Sun/Mon am) until
22.30; 52, Rue Lamarck (18th arr.);
Tel. 01 42 54 19 50; Métro: Lamarck-
Caulaincourt*

Buddha Bar (E3)
Trendy restaurant with Japanese-
American cuisine. A giant Buddha
watches over proceedings.
*Daily (except Sun lunchtime) until
24.00, bar until 02.00; 8, Rue Boissy
d'Anglas (8th arr.); Tel. 01 53 05 90
00; Métro: Concorde*

Closerie des Lilas (T) (F 6)

This classic restaurant is an institution in Montparnasse and is still a favourite meeting place for Parisian *intellos*. The Bar Américain is better value than the main establishment. Very smart.
Daily 12.00–02.00; 171, Boulevard du Montparnasse (6th arr.); Tel. 01 43 26 70 50; Métro: Vavin

Ledoyen (D 3)

Ghislaine Arabian creates gourmet dishes in her acclaimed restaurant off the Champs-Elysées.
1, Avenue Dutuit (8th arr.); Tel. 01 47 42 23 23; Métro: Champs-Elysées Clemenceau

Maxim's (E 3)

Heavenly surroundings, wicked prices. Even if the legendary Maxim's is no longer considered one of the gourmet temples of the world, eating here is still quite an experience.
3, Rue Royale (8th arr.); Tel. 01 42 65 27 94; Métro: Concorde

Procope (F 4)

This popular historic establishment in St-Germain, once an arena of revolutionary unrest, is the oldest café in Paris. Good food.
Daily 11.00–02.00; 13, Rue de l'Ancienne Comédie (6th arr.); Tel. 01 43 26 99 20; Métro: Odéon

Le Train Bleu (I 6)

★ Magnificent belle époque décor in the Gare de Lyon station. The food is excellent, especially the pâté de foie gras, lamb cutlets and salads. The prices are in keeping with the high quality.
Daily until 22.00; 20, Boulevard Diderot (Gare de Lyon, 1st floor) (12th arr.); Tel. 01 43 43 09 06; Métro: Gare de Lyon

Category 2
(From around 200 FF per person, including wine)

Bermuda Onion (A5)

Wonderful atmosphere, fashionable clientele and imaginative cuisine.
Daily, evenings only until 01.00, Sun brunch from 12.00; 16, Rue Linois (15th arr.); Tel. 01 45 75 11 11; Métro: Charles Michels

Café Marly (T) (F 3)

★ Next to the Pyramid, this café in the Louvre is ideal for some light refreshment before or after paying homage to the *Mona Lisa*. Haddock, pâté de foie gras and delicious cakes are just some of the menu items on offer.
Daily until 02.00; 93, Rue de Rivoli, Cour Napoleon-Louvre (1st arr.); Tel. 01 49 26 06 60; Métro: Palais Royal-Musée du Louvre

---

Say it with flowers

If you're lucky enough to be asked to someone's home in Paris, the invitation is quite likely to include an evening meal. Remember, it's a *faux pas* to arrive at the stated time – chances are the hosts won't be ready to receive you. It's customary to be about 15 minutes late and you should bring flowers, rather than a bottle of wine, leaving them wrapped, and with the label of a good florist clearly visible. Dinner, which tends to start rather formally, ends late and as a rule much more relaxed.

L'Escargot Montorgueil: a picture-book restaurant in Les Halles district

L'Escargot Montorgueil (T) (G 3)

Wonderful old restaurant in Les Halles district. Snails are the speciality. Advance booking essential.
Daily (except Sun/Mon) until 23.00; 38, Rue Montorgueil (1st arr.); Tel. 01 42 36 83 51; Métro: Etienne Marcel

Chez Georges (F 3)

Picturesque restaurant and bistro. Regular clientèle from the fashion and business world. French cuisine, excellent wine. The lunchtime menu changes daily.
Daily (except Sun); 1, Rue du Mail (2nd arr.); Tel. 01 42 60 07 11; Métro: Sentier

Jo Goldenberg (T) (H 4)

Lively establishment in the Jewish quarter of the Marais, reached via the delicatessen at the front (also good for a takeaway snack). Delicious eastern European specialities and occasional live music.
Daily until 24.00; 7, Rue des Rosiers (4th arr.); Tel. 01 48 87 20 16; Métro: St Paul

La Petite Chaise (E 4)

Claims to be the oldest restaurant in Paris. Excellent food.
Daily until 22.30; 36, Rue de Grenelle (7th arr.); Tel. 01 42 22 13 35; Métro: Rue du Bac

Pied de Cochon (T) (F 3)

Open round the clock, just as it used to be when the market halls were here, this unpretentious establishment offers good, traditional cuisine. Touristy, but not exclusively so – still a popular spot for Parisians to end an evening after the opera or theatre.
6, Rue de la Coquillière (1st arr.); Tel. 01 42 36 11 75; Métro: Les Halles

Thoumieux (D 4)

Stylish restaurant serving specialities from south-west France including cassoulet and a variety of duck-based dishes.
Daily until 24.00; 79, Rue St Dominique (7th arr.); Tel. 01 47 05 49 75; Métro: Latour Maubourg or Invalides

Category 3
(From around 100 FF per person, including wine)

Café des Beaux Arts (F 4)
⚚ When it comes to value for money, nothing in St-Germain-des-Prés beats this restaurant. Regular clientele from the nearby art school. Good, simple cooking and great atmosphere.
Daily until 23.00; 11, Rue Bonaparte (6th arr.); Tel. 01 43 26 92 64; Métro: St-Germain-des-Prés

Le Café de Commerce (B 5)
Large, spacious and very reasonable restaurant. Down-to-earth cooking in attractive surroundings. Outside terrace.
Daily until 24.00; 51, Rue du Commerce (15th arr.); Tel. 01 45 75 03 27; Métro: Emile Zola

Chartier (F 2)
⚚ There is always a crowd in this vast 100-year old restaurant. Old-fashioned, but the food is good and reasonably priced.
Daily 11.00-15.00 and 18.00-21.30; 7, Rue du Faubourg Montmartre (9th arr.); Tel. 01 47 70 86 29; Métro: Rue Montmartre

Le Drouot (F 3)
Unpretentious décor for unpretentious, good and reasonably priced food. Lively atmosphere.
Daily 12.00-15.00 and 18.00-22.00; 103, Rue de Richelieu (2nd arr.); Tel. 01 42 96 68 23; Métro: Richelieu Drouot

Hard Rock Café (F 2)
⚚ American food accompanied by rock music.
Daily until 02.00; 14, Boulevard Montmartre (9th arr.); Tel. 01 42 46 10 00; Métro: Rue Montmartre

L'Incroyable (F 3)
In a wonderful arcade in the Palais Royal. Simple, traditional cuisine. Pleasant atmosphere.
Closed Sat evng, Sun and Mon evng; 26, Rue de Richelieu (1st arr.); Tel. 01 42 96 24 64; Métro: Palais Royal

Le Nioullaville (I 2)
Large Chinese restaurant with very reasonably priced and good choice of specialities from Hong Kong. You can pick and choose from a number of dishes which are displayed on little trolleys.
Daily until 01.00; 32-34, Rue de l'Orillon (11th arr.); Tel. 01 43 38 95 23; Métro: Belleville

Perraudin (F 5)
Authentic bistro between the Panthéon and the Sorbonne, serving traditional cuisine. Good onion soup. Very reasonably priced. Popular with academics.
Daily (except Sun); 157, Rue St-Jacques (5th arr.); Tel. 01 46 33 15 75; Métro: Maubert Mutualité

Polidor (F 5)
★ This long-established budget bistro is popular with students and locals; the food is as good as ever. Many an illustrious figure has featured in its past list of regulars.
Daily (except Sun/Mon); 41, Rue Monsieur-le-Prince (6th arr.); Tel. 01 43 26 95 34; Métro: Odéon

Véro-Dodat (F 3)
You can eat well here in one of the loveliest arcades in Paris. Traditional cuisine is served in belle époque surroundings. If possible, get a table by the window with a view of the small shops.
Daily (except Sun) until 23.00; 19, Galerie Véro-Dodat (1st arr.); Tel. 01 45 08 92 06; Métro: Les Halles

The food and fashion capital

*From flea markets to haute couture,
Paris is a shopper's paradise*

Paris is a veritable shopper's paradise. The city streets are lined with a bewildering array of shops from elegant fashion boutiques, commercial art galleries, exclusive jewellers and enticing delicatessens, to bargain-basement stores, kitsch souvenir shops and every kind of specialist outlet you can imagine. While it is not a particularly cheap city, there are plenty of opportunities to pick up a bargain. The winter sales (*soldes*) start after Christmas and continue throughout January, and the summer sales run from mid-July until well into August. But you can find good deals and special offers outside the sales periods too. There are numerous cut-price stores known as *soldeurs permanents*, most of which stock last year's fashions, often designer labels (*dégriffé*), or slightly flawed items. Second-hand shops are a good source for original souvenirs and retro clothes (*fripes*), and early birds can always catch a good bargain at the flea markets.

The Galeries Lafayette is worth a visit just to admire its spectacular interior

Shops and department stores (*grands magasins*) are generally open Monday to Saturday from 09.00 or 09.30 until 18.30 or 19.00. Some of the smaller local shops still close for an hour at lunchtime. All the major department stores have one or two late night shopping days, and some shops even stay open around the clock. Many grocers (*épiceries*) and delicatessens (*traiteurs*) stay open late, except on Mondays when most food shops are closed. The Virgin Megastore on the Champs-Elysées, which has its own café, is open every day until midnight. The *drogueries* on the Champs-Elysées, near the Opéra, and in St-Germain-des-Prés, stay open until 02.00 and stock a wide range of goods including over-the-counter medication, international newspapers, gifts, food and cigarettes. Most of these drugstores have a café or restaurant attached, but they can be expensive.

Window shopping (or 'window licking' – *lécher les vitrines* – as the French call it) is a favourite Parisian pastime. You can fantasize about the jewellery displayed in the windows of the distinguished shops along the Rue de la Paix and the Place Vendôme; dream of furnishing your house with the art and antiques in the shops around St-Germain-des-Prés; and admire the fine crystal and ornaments in the Rue de Paradis, near the Gare de l'Est. The top *haute couture* houses are concentrated in the 'golden triangle' between Avenue Montaigne, the Champs-Elysées and Avenue Marceau, and most of them have boutiques in the elegant ★ Rue du Faubourg-St-Honoré. Younger fashion designers, such as Thierry Mugler, Jean-Paul Gaultier, and Kenzo, have congregated around ★ the Place des Victoires. St-Germain-des-Prés also has a good selection of more accessible designer boutiques, and the Forum shopping centres at Les Halles have a wide choice of reasonably-priced fashions. More recently, the Marais, between ★ Rue des Rosiers and Place des Vosges, has developed into something of a fashion mecca.

Credit cards can be used for payment in most outlets although some cards (Diners and American Express in particular) are less readily accepted because of the fees the vendor has to pay, while Eurocheques are rarely recognized.

ANTIQUARIAN BOOKSELLERS

Around 250 dealers in old books, maps, postcards posters and prints can be found by their little green stalls which line the left and right banks of the Seine between the Musée d'Orsay and the Ile de la Cité. You won't come across many bargains, but it's fun to browse and enjoy a typically Parisian scene.

ANTIQUES

Drouot Richelieu Auction House   (F 3)
★ If your French is up to it you can come here to bid, but it's not obligatory to participate. Auctions begin at 14.00.
Daily (except Sun); 9, Rue Drouot (9th arr.); Tel. 01 48 00 20 20; Métro: Richelieu Drouot

Village Saint Paul   (H 4)
Antiques, pictures, bric-a-brac and silverware in the backstreets of the Marais.
Daily; 23-27, Rue St-Paul (4th arr.); Métro: St Paul

Le Village Suisse   (C 5)
Around 200 antique dealers catering for sophisticated tastes. Near the Eiffel Tower.
Daily (except Tues/Wed) 11.00-19.00; 78, Avenue de Suffren (15th arr.); Métro: La Motte-Picquet Grenelle

ART GALLERIES

The more expensive, established galleries are found in the area around Avenue Matignon and Rue du Faubourg-St-Honoré. The St-Germain district is well known for its commercial galleries and there are a number of galleries specializing in modern art around the Pompidou Centre. Avant-garde art is concentrated in the Bastille district around the Rue de Lappe, Rue de la Roquette and the Rue de Charonne, and in the Marais district.

Viaduc des Arts   (I 5)
The arches beneath the disused railway line behind the Bastille Opéra have been lovingly restored and converted into art galleries,

MARCO POLO SELECTION: SHOPPING

1 Rue du Faubourg-St-Honoré
The place to find all the legendary names in haute couture (page 60)

2 Place des Victoires
Ready-to-wear fashions from the younger designer names (page 60)

3 Galeries Lafayette Haussmann
Everything your heart desires under one roof (page 62)

4 Rue Mouffetard
Colourful market street in the Latin Quarter (page 65)

5 Marché d'Aligre
The cheapest groceries in Paris (page 64)

6 Drouot Richelieu Auction House
Antiques and a free show (page 60)

7 Fauchon
A food-lover's temple (page 61)

8 Rue St-Placide
Soldes (sales) all year round (page 63)

9 Rue des Rosiers
Jewish specialities and trendy boutiques (page 60)

10 St-Ouen-Clignancourt flea market
Rows of stalls are crammed with antiques and bric-a-brac (page 64)

craft shops, restaurants and cafés.
Avenue Daumesnil (12th arr.); Métro: Bastille

CHOCOLATE & CONFECTIONERY

Debauve et Gallais   **(E 4)**
This former apothecary has been transformed into an exclusive chocolate shop. Smoothly coated sugared almonds (*dragées*), a sweet traditionally presented to wedding guests, are among their mouth-watering specialities. The shop itself is a historic building and is under preservation order.
30, Rue des Saints-Pères (7th arr.); Métro: St-Germain-des-Prés

Fouquet   **(C 2)**
Nothing but the best is stocked here. The sweets and pastries are heavenly, but don't come cheap.
22, Rue François I (8th arr.); Métro: Franklin-D.Roosevelt

DELICATESSENS

Chez Robert   **(G 2) and (O)**
Good quality pâté de foie gras packaged in pretty china containers (250 g to 1 kg), sausages and a wide range of home-made pies. Two branches.
Daily (except Sun afternoon and Mon); 50, Rue du Faubourg Saint-Denis (10th arr.); Métro: Strasbourg Saint Denis and 4, Rue Bayen (17th arr.); Métro: Ternes

Fauchon   **(E 2)**
★ The most famous food emporium in Paris. Just wander in and admire the luxury foods which are displayed like works of art – fresh exotic fruits, vegetables, teas, wines, pâtisseries, lobster, truffles, pâtés, cheeses, and a thousand other gourmet delights.
26, Place de la Madeleine (8th arr.); Métro: Madeleine

Gargantua (E 3)

Pâté de foie gras, delicious preserves and fine wines, all enticingly presented in this splendid shop, aptly named after the voracious hero of Rabelais' novel.
284, Rue St-Honoré (1st arr.); Métro: Tuileries

Goldenberg (H 4)

Excellent Jewish delicatessen with a restaurant at the back. Just one of the many Jewish speciality shops in the neighbourhood.
7, Rue des Rosiers (4th arr.); Métro: Saint Paul

Hédiard (E 2)

Luxury shop in the Fauchon mould, established nearly 150 years ago. Stocks the best of everything – fine teas, oils and vinegars, sweets and preserves etc. The French writer Colette was a regular customer. The adjacent restaurant is good but pricey.
21, Place de la Madeleine (8th arr.); Métro: Madeleine

Izraël (H 4)

Aladdin's cave of herbs, spices, and a variety of exotic foods from across the globe.
30, Rue François Miron (4th arr.); Métro: Saint Paul

Maxim's de Paris (D 2)

Pierre Cardin's 'boutique' for fine food. Many items can be sampled before buying, and everything comes beautifully wrapped.
76, Rue du Faubourg St-Honoré (8th arr.); Métro: Madeleine

Poilâne

Renowned throughout the country, the large, round sour-dough loaves are still made to the age-old family recipe. *Pain Poilâne* is at its best fresh from the wood-fired oven. The pâtisseries and apple pies are equally delicious. Two branches.
(E5) *8, Rue du Cherche Midi (6th arr.); Métro: St Sulpice, Sèvres Babylone*
(B5) *49, Boulevard de Grenelle (15th arr.); Métro: Dupleix*

Tang Frères (O)

Well-stocked Chinese grocery store in Chinatown.
Daily (except Mon) 09.00-19.00; 48, Avenue d'Ivry (13th arr.); Métro: Porte d'Ivry

DEPARTMENT STORES

Au Bon Marché (E 5)

❀ Founded in 1852, this precursor of the modern department store was the inspiration for Emile Zola's novel *Au Bonheur des Dames*. It's the best department store on the left bank of the Seine.
38, Rue de Sèvres (7th arr.); Métro: Sèvres-Babylone

Galeries Lafayette Haussmann (E 2)

★ ❀ The vast central hall with its huge glass dome is an architectural feat. Stocks all the big names from Gaultier, Rykiel, Ungaro, Mugler, and Agnes B. to Creeks and Fiorucci. Boasts the world's largest perfumery.
40, Boulevard Haussmann (9th arr.); Métro: Chaussée d'Antin

Le Printemps (E 2)

❀ The magnificent belle époque glass dome is under preservation order. All the big names in fashion and perfume under one roof. Fashion shows every Tuesday at 10.00 on the 6th floor. The café and terrace offer wonderful views.
64, Boulevard Haussmann (9th arr.); Métro: Havre Caumartin

La Samaritaine (F 4)

〰 ✿ 'You'll find the whole of Paris in La Samaritaine' – the store's well-worn slogan says it all. The biggest department store in Paris, it occupies three buildings along the river. You get a fantastic view of the Seine and the city centre from the summer terrace on the 10th floor.
Pont Neuf (on the Seine Quai, 1st arr.); Métro: Pont Neuf

DRUGSTORES

Newspapers, magazines, snacks, cigarettes, medicines and gifts.
(C2) *Daily 10.00-02.00; 133, Avenue des Champs-Elysées (8th arr.); Métro: Etoile*
(D3) *Daily 10.00-02.00; 1, Avenue Matignon (8th arr.); Métro: Franklin-D.Roosevelt*

FASHION

The dedicated fashion boutiques tend to be concentrated in certain districts and streets. Nearly all the *haute couture* houses are in and around the Avenue Montaigne (Chanel, Givenchy, Dior, Yves St Laurent), and you'll find expensive boutiques which stock the big-name designers in the Rue du Faubourg-St-Honoré (Gianni Versace, Hermès, Pierre Cardin, Karl Lagerfeld, Louis Féraud).

A new fashion centre has developed in the area in and around the Place des Victoires, where a number of exciting young *créateurs* have congregated. Thierry Mugler, Kenzo and Jean-Paul Gaultier are among the best-known names represented here. Gaultier's boutique in the Passage Vivienne is also worth a look. You can find a number of good fashion boutiques in St-Germain-des-Prés – Place St-Sulpice being home to the most elegant. The more avant-garde designers are found in the Rue du Cherche Midi, while the more formal fashions are in Rue de Rennes.

An increasing number of interesting designers are setting up shop in the Marais (such as Lolita Lempicka in the Rue des Rosiers and Azzedine Alaïa in the Rue de Moussy), and the Bastille area is full of trendy boutiques. The widest range of ready-to-wear fashions can be found in the Forum des Halles (see p. 29).

Most fashion designers sell their previous year's collections at cut-price rates in the so-called *stocks*. (Rue d'Alésia in the 14th *arrondissement* is known as 'the street of the *stocks*' – Métro: Alésia, Plaisance). Reasonably-priced designer seconds are known as *dé-griffé*. Watch for the *soldeurs* in the ★ Rue St-Placide *(6th arr.)*.

Basic Dressing (F 3)

Cut-price designer wear by the Place des Victoires.
10, Rue Hérold (1st arr.); Métro: Louvre-Rivoli

Halle By's (F 2)

Big names, affordable prices.
60, Rue de Richelieu (2nd arr.); Métro: Bourse

Réciproque (A 3)

Nearly-new designer-label clothing at bargain prices.
89-123, Rue de la Pompe (16th arr.); Métro: Rue de la Pompe

Soldeurs (various designers) (E 2)

Annexe des Créateurs.
19, Rue Godot du Mauroy (9th arr.); Métro: Madeleine

Marché d'Aligre (I 5)

★ ☺ This authentic Parisian market, not far from the Bastille Opéra, is one of the liveliest markets in the city. The stalls are piled high with fruit and vegetables, fish and meat, cheese, herbs and spices, alongside clothes, hardware, kitchen utensils and bric-a-brac. There are plenty of bars and cafés in the neighbourhood.

Daily, mornings (except Mon); Place Aligre (12th arr.); Métro: Ledru Rollin

Puces de la Porte de Montreuil (O)

Lovely sprawling market selling all sorts of junk, bric-a-brac and second-hand goods. Best to go early in the morning.

Sat, Sun, Mon 06.30-18.00; Métro: Porte de Montreuil

Puces de St-Ouen-Clignancourt (O)

★ ⚡ Made up of various different markets, this labyrinth of around 1500 stalls on the northern outskirts of the city is said to be the largest flea market in Europe. An enormous choice of goods, ranging from high-quality antiques to cheap junk. When you come out of the métro station you have to make your way past a number of stalls selling cheap, shoddy goods before you get to the markets proper. The area is dotted with bars and cafés for a much-needed break.

Sat/Sun/Mon 08.00-19.00; Métro: Porte de Clignancourt (18th arr.)

Puces de Vanves (O)

⚡ Bric-a-brac, furniture and junk. At its best in the morning.

Sat/Sun 09.00-18.00; Avenue Georges Lafenestre-Rue Marc Sangnier (14th arr.); Métro: Porte de Vanves

The Rue du Faubourg-St-Honoré: the heart of Parisian haute couture

Carrousel du Louvre (F 3)

The new underground shopping complex in the Louvre has about 30 upmarket shops offering a wide choice of quality gifts and souvenirs. Not cheap, but not too over-priced either.

Daily, except Tues, 10.00-20.00; 99, Rue de Rivoli (1st arr.); Métro: Palais Royal-Musée du Louvre

Museum Shops

Like the Louvre, the Musée d'Orsay and many of the other museums have their own shops on the premises selling books, postcards, posters, souvenirs, and other articles thematically connected to the objects on display.

JEWELLERY

All the big names in jewellery are dotted around Place Vendôme and Rue de la Paix – Cartier, Chaumet, Boucheron, Van Cleef & Arpels, and the famous silver cutlery maker, Christofle.

MARKETS

Every district in Paris has its own market once or twice a week. There are also a number of market streets which are active six days a week.

Boulevard de Belleville (O)
Exotic, colourful, cheap.
Tues and Fri 09.00-13.00; Métro: Belleville (20th arr.)

Rue de Buci (F 4)
❀ In St-Germain-des-Prés; really busy at weekends.
Daily 09.00-13.00 and 16.00-19.00; Métro: Mabillon (6th arr.)

Rue Daguerre (O)
❀ Authentic produce market in Montparnasse.
Daily (except Mon); Métro: Denfert Rochereau (14th arr.)

Rue des Martyrs (F 1)
❀ Picturesque market at the foot of Montmartre.
Daily (except Mon); Métro: Pigalle (9th arr.)

Rue Mouffetard (G 6)
★ Lively market street with African section. Touristy but fun.
Daily (except Mon); Métro: Censier Daubenton (15th arr.)

Marché St-Pierre (F 1)
An inspiring choice of affordable textiles. In Montmartre.

Daily (except Sun/Mon) 09.30-18.00; 2, Rue Charles Nodier (18th arr.); Métro: Anvers

MUSIC

FNAC
Good selection of CDs, tapes and books at discounted prices. Theatre and concert tickets also available. Several branches.
(G3) *Forum des Halles, Level 2 (1st arr.); Métro: Châtelet Les Halles*
(E5) *136, Rue de Rennes (6th arr.); Métro: Rennes, St Placide*
(C2) *26, Avenue de Wagram (17th arr.); Métro: Etoile*

Virgin in the Carrousel (F 3)
Enormous choice of music and books in the new Louvre shopping complex. Open Sundays.
Métro: Tuileries, Palais Royal (1st arr.)

Virgin Megastore (C 2)
⚓ Vast store with listening posts and a café. Open until midnight.
52-60 Avenue des Champs-Elysées (8th arr.); Métro: Franklin-D. Roosevelt

PERFUME

Paris Look (F 3)
13, Avenue de l'Opéra (1st arr.); Métro: Opéra

Michel Swiss (E 2)
16, Rue de la Paix, 2nd floor (2nd arr.); Métro: Opéra

STAMPS

Marché aux Timbres (D 2-3)
Vintage stamps and postcards.
Thurs, Sat, Sun, public holidays; Champs-Elysées at the corner of Avenue Marigny and Gabriel (8th arr.); Métro: Champs-Elysées Clemenceau

A good night's sleep

Whether you want to stay in a luxurious palace or a bohemian garret room, the city's 1400 hotels cater for every need

A night in one of the legendary grand 'palace' hotels such as the Crillon, the Ritz, the Bristol, the Meurice or the Plaza Athénée is something most of us can only dream about. But Paris offers an astounding range of alternatives. With over 1400 hotels to choose from, there is accommodation to suit every pocket. Most of the luxury hotels are found in the fashion and business districts on the right bank of the Seine. The smaller hotels, renowned for their charm and character, tend to be located on the Left Bank, in the Latin Quarter or around St-Germain-des-Prés, or else on the Ile-St-Louis and in the Marais district. The better places do tend to get booked up weeks ahead, so it is advisable to make your reservations well in advance. If you don't manage to book a room beforehand, however, the *Office du Tourisme et des Congrès de Paris* (**D 3**) (*127, Avenue des Champs-Elysées, Tel. 01 49 52 53 54*) will help you find somewhere to stay. A small fee is charged for this service, and the accommodation is guaranteed for one night only. Most hotels will make reservations over the phone, but your booking is only really guaranteed on receipt of a letter or fax. Some hotels will ask for your credit card number. Those that do not accept credit cards may request an international money order as a deposit.

The average Parisian hotel offers double and twin rooms. Single rooms are rare, and not much cheaper. By law, tariffs have to be displayed at reception and in your room, and they are always quoted per person. Prices vary considerably, depending on the time of year and the district. For those on a tight budget, basic accommodation can be found for as little as 100 FF, while for a few hundred francs a night you can find a comfortable, even romantic place to stay.

Hotels are rated according to strict criteria from one to four star. Broadly speaking, one star is for good basic accommodation, a two-star hotel has more facilities such as en suite shower and

The Crillon on Place de la Concorde is one of the finest hotels in town

MARCO POLO SELECTION: HOTELS

1 Angleterre
Old-fashioned charm in
St-Germain (page 69)

2 Pavillon de la Reine
Haven of peace on the
picturesque Place des Vosges
(page 69)

3 Tim Hôtel Montmartre
Romantic hotel on a tree-
lined square (page 72)

4 Hôtel des Grandes Ecoles
Rural calm in the bustling
Latin Quarter (page 70)

5 La Louisiane
Legendary hotel, popular
with writers (page 69)

6 Solférino
Distinguished hotel near
Musée d'Orsay (page 72)

7 Istria
Lovely location in the heart
of Montparnasse (page 70)

8 Récamier
Peaceful hotel by the Luxembourg Gardens (page 70)

9 Prima Lepic
A touch of the Bohemian on
Montmartre (page 72)

**10 Le Relais Hôtel du
Vieux Paris**
Luxury in the Latin Quarter
(page 70)

toilet, a three-star hotel should be very comfortable, with good facilities, and four-star is luxury class. However, standards do differ widely between establishments.

Breakfast is not usually included in the room price but it's best to check in advance. It is fairly standard – white coffee, white bread, usually a piece of *baguette,* with jam or marmalade, or perhaps a croissant. If you want more you generally have to pay for it. Tea is available in most places, but will invariably be served with a slice of lemon. You have to specify if you want milk (*lait*). If breakfast is not included, you may find that you are better off going to a local café, unless of course you prefer the luxury of having it in your room.

The hotels recommended here have been classified into three categories: budget and basic, medium-priced with certain facilities, and upper price range

bordering on the luxury class. For the budget hotels (Category C) you should expect to pay from 250 FF for a double room. It's very seldom less than that. For the medium-priced hotels (Category B) you'll not find much under 400 FF, and for the higher priced hotels (Category A) expect to pay upwards of 500 FF.

A list of youth hostels and cheap accommodation for young people has also been included. Paris certainly offers more and usually better accommodation in this category than most other large cities.

The so-called *palaces* may be beyond most people's means, but you can still treat yourself to a little taste of luxury. Go for a late-night drink at the Hemingway Bar in the Ritz or pop into the Plaza Athénée, where you can enjoy tea with musical accompaniment. Breakfast at the Crillon is affordable and unforgettable.

CATEGORY A

(From 500 FF per person)

Abbaye Saint-Germain (E 5)
Peace and luxury in a converted monastery. 26 rooms.
10, Rue Cassette (6th arr.); Tel. 01 45 44 38 11, Fax 01 45 48 07 86; Métro: St Sulpice

Angleterre (F 4)
★ Comfortable rooms in the former British Embassy, renowned for its beautiful staircase which is under preservation order. In the heart of St-Germain. 26 rooms.
44, Rue Jacob (6th arr.); Tel. 01 42 60 34 72, Fax 01 42 60 16 93; Métro: St-Germain-des-Prés

Hôtel Burgundy (E 3)
Quiet and elegant hotel, a short walk from the Louvre. Parking. 90 rooms.
8, Rue Duphot (8th arr.); Tel. 01 42 60 34 12, Fax 01 47 03 95 20; Métro: Madeleine

Colbert (G 5)
Charming 18th-century building. Some of the rooms have a view of Notre-Dame. 38 rooms.
7, Rue de l'Hôtel Colbert (5th arr.); Tel. 01 43 25 85 65, Fax 01 43 25 80 19; Métro: Maubert Mutualité

L'Hôtel (F 4)
Oscar Wilde spent his last days here. Ornate interior – all marble, silk, art deco and kitsch – a small garden and busy bar. The two suites overlooking St-Germain are sought after and usually booked, but the smaller rooms are just as stylish. 25 rooms/2 suites.
13, Rue des Beaux-Arts (6th arr.); Tel. 01 43 25 27 22, Fax 01 43 25 64 81; Métro: St-Germain-des-Prés

La Louisiane (F 4)
★ A St-Germain legend overlooking the lively Rue du Buci market. Art deco interior. Comfortable. 80 rooms.
60, Rue de Seine (6th arr.); Tel. 01 43 29 59 30; Fax 01 46 34 23 87; Métro: St-Germain-des-Prés

Les Marronniers (F 4)
The two chestnut trees after which the hotel is named stand in the delightful hidden garden. The hotel is filled with plants and flowers, and you can breakfast on the veranda. 37 rooms.
21, Rue Jacob (6th arr.); Tel. 01 43 25 30 60, Fax 01 40 46 83 56; Métro: St-Germain-des-Prés

Pavillon de la Reine (H 4)
★ Luxury hotel on the Place des Vosges in the heart of the Marais. 53 small but sumptuous rooms. Garage.
28, Place des Vosges (4th arr.); Tel. 01 42 77 96 40, Fax 01 42 77 63 06; Métro: Saint Paul

Relais Christine (F 4)
This expensive but very elegant hotel is set in the cloister of a converted 16th-century abbey in the heart of St-Germain. Beautifully modernized and renovated. Peaceful and romantic. 51 rooms.
3, Rue Christine (6th arr.); Tel. 01 43 26 71 80, Fax 01 43 26 89 38; Métro: Mabillon

Saint-Louis (H 5)
The old paintings and antique furniture add to the character and charm of this lovely hotel. But rooms are small and there is no lift. 25 rooms.
75, Rue St-Louis-en-l'Ile (4th arr.); Tel. 01 46 34 04 80, Fax 01 46 34 02 13; Métro: Pont Marie

Saints-Pères (E 4)

Traditional hotel in a renovated mansion with its own garden. Popular with American writers, who like to meet their publishers at the bar. 40 rooms.

65, Rue des Saints-Pères (6th arr.); Tel. 01 45 44 50 00; Métro: St-Germain-des-Prés

Le Relais Hôtel du Vieux Paris (G 5)

★ Luxury and charm in a wonderfully-renovated historic building. 21 rooms.

9, Rue Git-le-Coeur (6th arr.); Tel. 01 43 54 41 66, Fax 01 43 26 00 15; Métro: St Michel

CATEGORY B

(From 400 FF per person)

Hôtel de Beaune (E 4)

Peaceful and stylish hotel in the heart of St-Germain. Friendly reception. Garage nearby. 19 rooms.

29, Rue de Beaune (7th arr.); Tel. 01 42 61 24 89, Fax 01 49 27 02 12; Métro: Rue du Bac

Chopin (F 2)

Old-fashioned dream of a hotel in a pretty passageway near the *Grands Boulevards*. Next door to the Grévin Wax Museum. Very romantic. 38 rooms.

46, Passage Jouffroy (9th arr.); Tel. 01 47 70 58 10, Fax 01 42 47 00 70; Métro: Rue Montmartre

Hôtel de Deux Acacias (B 2)

On a quiet street in a smart residential area. Some of the rooms can accommodate three people. 31 rooms.

28, Rue de l'Arc de Triomphe (17th arr.); Tel. 01 43 80 01 81; Fax 01 40 53 94 62; Métro: Charles de Gaulle-Etoile

Esmeralda (G 5)

Medieval house in the bustling Latin Quarter. Slightly tatty, but full of character. Splendid views of Notre-Dame. There is a pair of small cheap rooms under the rafters. 19 rooms.

4, Rue St-Julien-le-Pauvre (5th arr.); Tel. 01 43 54 19 20, Fax 01 40 51 00 68; Métro: St Michel

Hôtel des Grandes Ecoles (G 6)

★ Romantic hotel in the heart of the Latin Quarter, spread across three houses that share a garden. The rooms are attractively furnished, and the atmosphere is friendly. Good value. 48 rooms.

75, Rue du Cardinal Lemoine (5th arr.); Tel. 01 43 26 79 23, Fax 01 43 25 28 15; Métro: Cardinal Lemoine, Place Monge

Istria (E 6)

★ Picabia and Kiki de Montparnasse once lived in this comfortable hotel which has lost none of its character. Next door to an artist's studio in the heart of Montparnasse. 26 rooms.

29, Rue Campagne Première (14th arr.); Tel. 01 43 20 91 82, Fax 01 43 22 48 45; Métro: Raspail

Hôtel de la Place des Vosges (H 4)

Beautifully restored building overlooking the loveliest square in Paris. Tastefully decorated rooms with shower. 16 rooms.

12, Rue Birague (4th arr.); Tel. 01 42 72 60 46, Fax 01 42 72 02 64; Métro: Saint Paul

Récamier (F 5)

★ Old-fashioned charm in a great location. 30 rooms.

3, Place St-Sulpice (6th arr.); Tel. 01 43 26 04 89, Fax 01 46 33 27 73; Métro: St Sulpice

Parisian Palaces

Le Bristol (D 2)

They don't come any more luxurious than this. Near the Elysée Palace, this hotel is popular with visitors of State. Restaurant with garden. 195 rooms and suites. From 2500 FF.

12, Rue du Faubourg-St-Honoré (8th arr.); Tel. 01 53 43 43 00, Fax 01 53 43 43 26; Métro: Miromesnil

Crillon (E 3)

Grand hotel, magnificently restored. The wonderful façade dates from the 18th century and the restaurant in gold and marble has one of the best kitchens in Paris. 210 rooms and suites. From 2000 FF.

10, Place de la Concorde (8th arr.); Tel. 01 44 71 15 00, Fax 01 43 71 15 02; Métro: Concorde

Hôtel San Regis (C 3)

Small but stylish hotel with tastefully-decorated rooms. Near the Avenue Montaigne. 44 rooms. From 2000 FF.

12, Rue Jean-Goujon (8th arr.); Tel. 01 44 95 16 16, Fax 01 45 61 05 48; Métro: George V

Meurice (E3)

Old-fashioned style with modern comforts. Salvador Dali lived here for a while. Near the Tuileries. 200 rooms and apartments. From 1500 FF.

228, Rue de Rivoli (1st arr.); Tel. 01 44 58 10 10, Fax 01 44 58 10 17; Métro: Tuileries

Plaza Athénée (C 3)

Luxury hotel renowned for its first-class service. A favourite among film stars, royalty and fashion designers. 250 rooms and apartments. From 2200 FF.

25, Avenue Montaigne (8th arr.); Tel. 01 47 23 78 33, Fax 01 47 20 20 70; Métro: Franklin-D. Roosevelt

Résidence Maxim's (D 3)

Hotel next to the Elysée Palace, owned by Pierre Cardin. Decorated with exquisite taste and at great expense. Much of the valuable period furniture comes from his own private collection. 250 rooms and apartments. A night here can set you back as much as 30 000 FF.

42, Avenue Gabriel (8th arr.); Tel. 01 45 61 96 33, Fax 01 42 89 06 07; Métro: Champs-Elysées Clemenceau

Ritz (E 3)

Coco Chanel lived here and Ernest Hemingway made full use of the bar. Millionaires and princes love the opulence and comfort of this hotel. Luxury health centre. 200 suites and rooms. From 2000 FF.

15, Place Vendôme (1st arr.); Tel. 01 42 60 38 30, Fax 01 42 86 00 91; Métro: Opéra

La Villa (F 4)

The stark modern interiors of this luxury hotel in St-Germain are bright, elegant and refreshing, though it may not appeal to more traditional tastes. 31 rooms. From 650 FF.

29, Rue Jacob (6th arr.); Tel. 01 43 26 60 00, Fax 01 46 34 63 63; Métro: St-Germain-des-Prés

Hôtel du Septième Art (H 4)

A small hotel in the Marais ideal for film fans. It is decorated with film posters, black and white photos and other movie memorabilia. Near the Village de St Paul and a short walk from the Seine. Two studios at the top are available for short term rent. 23 rooms.
20, Rue St-Paul (4th arr.); Tel. 01 42 77 04 03, Fax 01 42 77 69 10; Métro: St Paul, Pont Marie

Solférino (E 4)

★ Quiet, old-fashioned comfort in friendly surroundings. Breakfast veranda. Central. 34 rooms.
91, Rue de Lille (7th arr.); Tel. 01 47 05 85 54, Fax 01 45 55 51 16; Métro: Solférino

Tim Hôtel Montmartre (F 1)

★ Next to the legendary Bateau Lavoir studios, where Picasso, Max Ernst and many other artists lived and worked. Superb views from the upper floors. 51 rooms.
11, Place Emile Goudeau (18th arr.); Tel. 01 42 55 74 79, Fax 01 42 55 71 01; Métro: Abbesses

Vieux Marais (G 3)

30 basic, comfortable rooms on 5 floors, with flowered wallpaper.
8, Rue du Plâtre (4th arr.); Tel. 01 42 78 47 22, Fax 01 42 78 34 22; Métro: Rambuteau

CATEGORY C

(From 250 FF per person)

Hôtel des Académies (E 6)

Basic and clean. Excellent location in Montparnasse. 21 rooms.
15, Rue de la Grande Chaumière (6th arr.); Tel. 01 43 26 66 44, Fax 01 43 26 03 72; Métro: Vavin, RER: Port Royal

Hôtel des Alliés (G 6)

Simple hotel in the student district, not far from the Jardin des Plantes. 45 rooms.
20, Rue Berthollet (5th arr.); Tel. 01 43 31 47 52, Fax 01 45 35 13 92; Métro: Censier Daubenton

Camélia (O)

Cheap, basic, but clean hotel. Not particularly central. 20 rooms.
6, Avenue Philippe Auguste (11th arr.); Tel. 01 43 73 67 50, no Fax; Métro: Nation

Hôtel de Chevreuse (E 6)

Peaceful hotel in Montparnasse, within easy reach of cinemas, cafés and Luxembourg Gardens. Very good value. 22 rooms.
3, Rue de Chevreuse (6th arr.); Tel. 01 43 20 93 16, Fax. 43 21 43 72; Métro: Vavin

Hôtel de Nesle (F 4)

In the middle of St-Germain. Original rooms, small garden. Reasonably priced. No advance booking. 20 rooms.
7, Rue de Nesle (6th arr.); Tel. 01 43 54 62 41, no Fax; Métro: Odéon

Prima Lepic (F 1)

★ Bohemian hotel in Montmartre. Comfortable, with pretty rooms hung with bright cheerful wallpaper. Some of the rooms can accommodate four people. Short walk to Sacré-Coeur. 38 rooms.
29, Rue Lepic (18th arr.); Tel. 01 46 06 44 64, Fax 01 46 06 66 11; Métro: Blanche

Saint-André-des-Arts (F 4)

Inexpensive rooms in a charming 17th-century building. Busy.
66, Rue Saint-André-des-Arts (6th arr.); Tel. 01 43 26 96 16, Fax 01 43 29 73 34; Métro: Odéon

ALTERNATIVE ACCOMMODATION

Accueil France Famille (O)
Bed and breakfast in a French family home. Advance booking essential. 1 week: 1250 FF.
5, Rue François Coppée (15th arr.); Tel. 01 45 54 22 39; Fax 01 45 58 43 25; Métro: Boucicaut

Paris Bienvenue (C 2)
Accommodation ranging from single rooms to luxury flats. Above the *Office du Tourisme et des Congrès, 127, Av. des Champs Elysées (8th arr.); Tel. 01 49 52 53 54, Fax 01 49 52 53 00; Métro: George V*

Parissimo (D 4)
Studios or apartments with service from 400 FF.
9, Avenue de la Motte-Picquet (7th arr.); Tel. 01 45 51 11 11, Fax 01 45 55 55 81; Métro: Latour Maubourg

BUDGET & STUDENT

Accueil des Jeunes de France (AJF)
Over 8000 cheap rooms for around 100 FF per night. No advance booking, but a bed for the night is guaranteed. All three hostels are centrally located:
(G4) Beaubourg, next to the Pompidou Centre, *119, Rue St Martin (4th arr.); Tel. 01 42 77 87 80; Métro: Rambuteau, Châtelet Les Halles, Hôtel de Ville*
(F6) Latin Quarter, *139, Boulevard St-Michel (5th arr.); Tel. 01 43 54 95 86; Métro: St Michel*
(G1) Gare du Nord, *Nouvelle Gare Banlieue (10th arr.); Tel. 01 42 85 86 19; Métro: Gare du Nord*

Centre International de Séjour de Paris (CISP) (O)
Hotel with swimming pool.
6, Avenue Maurice Ravel (12th arr.);

Tel/Fax 01 43 43 19 01; Métro: Porte de Vincennes

Crous-Academie de Paris (F 6)
39, Av. de G. Bernanos (5th arr.); Tel. 01 40 51 36 00; Métro/RER: Port Royal

Le Fauconnier (H 4)
Old palais in the Marais. 120 FF.
11, Rue du Fauconnier (4th arr.); Tel. 01 42 74 23 45, Fax 01 40 27 81 64; Métro: Saint Paul, Pont Marie

Le Fourcy (H 4)
Restored Marais mansion. Rooms with shower sleep 2 or 4. 220 beds. 120 FF.
6, Rue de Fourcy (4th arr.); Tel. 01 42 74 23 45, Fax 01 40 27 81 64; Métro: Pont Marie

Foyer International d'Accueil de Paris (FIAP) (O)
Comfortable rooms sleep 1 to 5.
30, Rue Cabanis (14th arr.); Tel. 01 45 89 89 15, Fax 01 45 89 10 58; Métro: Glacière

Le Jules Ferry (youth hostel) (H 3)
Lights out at 01.00.
8, Boulevard Jules Ferry (11th arr.); Tel. 01 43 57 55 60, Fax 01 40 21 79 92; Métro: République

Mike's Hostel (H 1)
Cheap, basic accommodation in a lively area. From 75 FF per night in summer.
122, Bd. de la Chapelle (18th arr.); Tel. 01 42 23 45 64, Fax 01 42 23 54 24; Métro: Barbès Rochechouart

Halls of Residence (university accommodation) (O)
Rooms for rent in vacations.
Cité Universitaire; 19, Boulevard Jourdan (14th arr.); Tel. 01 45 89 68 52, no Fax; RER: Cité Universitaire

Paris diary

The cultural calendar is full all year round

Whatever the season, there is always some event, festival or celebration going on in Paris. The activities begin to build up in the early spring when the city starts to come back to life after a brief period of winter calm.

In March, the largest funfair in Paris, the *Foire du Trône*, is set up in the Bois de Vincennes. Labour Day is celebrated on 1 May throughout the city, but particularly in the working-class districts where crowds of people march through the streets, and little bunches of lily of the valley are sold on street corners to celebrate the coming of spring. The ★ *Fête de la Musique*, which is held on midsummer's night, gets bigger, louder and more colourful every year. The whole city, it seems, pours onto the streets, and music is played throughout the night.

On the evening of 13 July, the eve of Bastille Day, firemen's balls are traditionally organized across the city. People dance down by

the Seine and in the streets. Many Parisians, however, prefer to escape to the country. On Bastille Day itself, a traditional military parade is held along the Champs-Elysées, and the highlight of the evening is the grand fireworks display on the Place du Trocadéro. *Le Quatorze Juillet* (14 July) also marks the beginning of the summer 'shutdown'. Many of the local shops shut for the holidays, and for the whole of August the streets are relatively free of traffic. For the benefit of the tourists, however, concerts and cultural events are held in churches and parks throughout the summer.

After the long summer break, the calendar of cultural and social events is full until the end of the year. The largest of these is the Autumn Festival – an exciting programme of international theatre, music and dance productions.

11 November is a more sombre occasion, when the 1918 Armistice is celebrated and the victims of both world wars are remembered. The President and Prime Minister lay wreaths at the Tomb of the Unknown Soldier at the Arc de Triomphe.

Street entertainers, pictured here in St-Germain, perform on squares and street corners all over the city

During the Christmas period, all the main streets are festooned with lights. The most spectacular ★ illuminations can be seen on the Avenue Montaigne and the Rue du Faubourg St-Honoré, on the Grands Boulevards, by the Opéra, and along the Champs-Elysées. Cafés, restaurants, theatres, and cinemas are all open during the Christmas holidays (*Les Fêtes*), and festive menus in the bistros and restaurants add to the sense of occasion. Christmas itself is a quiet family affair while New Year's Eve ★ (*Le Réveillon*) is celebrated with gusto. Fireworks crackle through the whole city, and there is plenty of activity and general mayhem.

PUBLIC HOLIDAYS

1 January
Easter Sunday
Easter Monday
1 May *(May Day/Labour Day)*
8 May *(VE Day)*
Ascension Day *(40 days after Easter)*
Whitsun *(7th Sunday after Easter)*
Whit Monday
14 July *(Bastille Day)*
15 August *(Assumption of the Virgin Mary)*
1 November *(All Saints' Day)*
11 November *(Armistice Day 1918)*
25 December

Most museums are closed on public holidays, but a number of shops and restaurants stay open.

SPECIAL EVENTS

January
Last Sunday in the month: *Prix d'Amérique* trotting race. *Hippodrome des Vincennes in the Bois de Vincennes; Métro: St-Mandé Tourelle, Porte Dorée* (**O**)

March/June
Late March to early June: 🏃 ☻
Foire du Trône: the largest funfair in France. (**O**) *Pelouse de Reuilly, Bois de Vincennes*

April
10-20 April: Large flea market in the Bastille. (**H5**) *Daily 11.00-19.00; Métro: Bastille (12th arr.)*
Last Sunday in April: The Paris Marathon. *Starts around 09.00 on the Champs-Elysées*

May
1-15 May: Antiques Fair. Dealers display their wares on street stalls in St-Germain-des-Prés. (**F4**) *Carré Rive Gauche (6th arr.)*
May to October: Water and music displays in the grounds of Versailles. (**O**) *Every Sun at 15.30*
Mid-May to end June: *Festival de Paris*. Concerts, dance, opera and other performances. *Held in various churches, concert halls, theatres and streets.*
22 May: *Fête de la Jeunesse*. Free concerts and events throughout the city.
Last week in May and first week in June: French Tennis Open. (**O**) *Stade Roland Garros; Bois de Boulogne; Métro: Porte d'Auteuil (16th arr.)*

June
8-30 June: Festival of St-Germain in St-Germain-des-Prés. Exhibitions, music, theatre and markets. (**F5**) *Place St-Sulpice (6th arr.); Métro: St Sulpice*
9-30 June: *Festival de la Butte Montmartre.* Theatre, classical music and dance. *Métro: Abbesses, Anvers, Jules Joffrin (18th arr.)*
Mid-June to mid-July: *Les Fêtes du Marais*. Concerts, balls, plays, exhibitions. (**H4**) *Métro: St Paul (4th arr.)*

MARCO POLO SELECTION: EVENTS

1 New Year's Eve – *Réveillon*
Raucous celebrations throughout the city (page 76)

2 La Fête de la Musique
Music and street entertainment on midsummer's night (pages 75 and 77)

3 Bastille Day
Dancing, parades and fireworks to celebrate the French national holiday (page 77)

4 Versailles
Music and fireworks against a magnificent palatial backdrop (page 77)

5 Montmartre wine festival
Popular street festival to celebrate the grape harvest (page 77)

6 Christmas illuminations
At their most impressive on the Champs-Elysées (page 76)

---

21 June: ★ ⚘ ❀ *Fête de la Musique.* Hundreds of musical performances all over Paris.
27-29 June: ⚘ ❀ *Fête du Cinéma.* Cheap films in all cinemas.

July
Early July to mid-August: Annual fair in the Tuileries Gardens. (**E3**) *12.00-24.00; Métro: Tuileries (1st arr.)*
13 and 14 July: ★ ❀ Bastille Day.
Mid-July to mid-August: *Paris, Quartier d'Eté.* Theatre, music, dance, film. *Garnier Opéra, Jardins de Luxembourg, Parc de la Villette, Théâtre Chaillot*
Penultimate Sunday: *Tour de France* ends on the Champs-Elysées. (**C2**) *Métro: Franklin-D. Roosevelt (8th arr.)*

September
★ First and second Saturdays: Water and firework displays, live performances and music at Versailles. (**O**)
20 September: Autumn Festival begins. Plays, concerts and exhibitions until the end of the year.
3rd weekend: *Journée du Patrimoine.* Free entrance to museums and monuments, many of which are usually closed to the public.

October
8 October-24 December: *Festival d'Art Sacré de la Ville de Paris.* Concerts in churches and synagogues, in the *Théâtre des Champs-Elysées* (**C3**) and the *Salle Pleyel* (**C1**).
First Saturday: ★ Montmartre wine festival. (**O**) *Corner of Rue des Saules and Rue St-Vincent (18th arr.); Métro: Lamarck Caulaincourt*
Mid-October: *FIAC* – International Fair of Contemporary Art. (**D3**) *Grand Palais (8th arr.); Métro: Champs-Elysées Clemenceau*
Mid-October: *La Genie de la Bastille.* Artists in the area open their studios to the public. *Information kiosk on Place de la Bastille (12th arr.)* (**I5**); *Métro: Bastille*
Mid- to end October: ⚘ *Festival de Jazz de Paris.* International jazz musicians play in clubs across Paris. Main venues: *Auditorium des Halles (1st arr.)* (**G3**) and *Théâtre de la Ville (4th arr.)* (**G4**)

November
November and December: International Dance Festival. *Centre Beaubourg-Pompidou (4th arr.)* (**G4**) and *Théâtre des Champs-Elysées (8th arr.)* (**C3**)

Out on the town

A guide to theatres and concerts, revues and discos, cabarets and French folk, jazz and cinema, in a city that never sleeps

Paris is one of the world's great entertainment capitals. This becomes obvious the minute you look through any of the listings magazines. The choice of venues and events on offer is overwhelming. Every evening, some 200 plays, operas, ballets and contemporary dance performances are staged. Paris is home to a number of prestigious orchestras, which means there is always an opportunity to see a good classical concert. All the latest films are on release (many in English with French subtitles) in the city's countless cinemas. There are cabarets and revues, nightclubs and discos, jazz clubs and music halls all over the city.

Most of the entertainment venues and well-known Parisian hang-outs are concentrated in specific areas, namely St-Germain-des-Prés and the Latin Quarter, Montparnasse, the Les Halles district and the Marais, Montmartre, the Champs-Elysées, the Grands Boulevards and the Bastille.

Glitz and glamour at the Folies Bergères

BARS

Le Café de la Plage   (I 5)
A lively, friendly bar with a jazz club in the basement. In the Bastille district.
Jazz club closed Sun/Mon; Bar daily; 59, Rue de Charonne (11th arr.); Tel. 01 47 00 91 60; Métro: Bastille

China Club   (I 5)
Popular hang-out for the young and trendy in the Bastille district. Good cocktails. Bar and restaurant serving Chinese food.
Daily until 02.00; 50, Rue de Charenton (12th arr.); Tel. 01 43 43 82 02; Métro: Bastille

Closerie des Lilas   (F 6)
Legendary late-night piano bar. Brass plaques on the tables mark where Hemingway and other great literary figures used to sit. Good cocktails and nice big pavement terrace.
Daily 10.00-02.00; 171, Boulevard du Montparnasse (6th arr.); Métro: Raspail

Le Dépanneur   (F 1)
✠ American bar near Pigalle. Tex-Mex and Tequila. A regular haunt

for night owls – one of the few bars which stays open round the clock. Gets crowded at weekends.
27, Rue Fontaine (9th arr.); Métro: Pigalle, Blanche

L'Entre Pots (I 5)

⚘ Another trendy bar in the Bastille district. Great décor.
Daily 19.00-01.30; 14, Rue de Charonne (11th arr.); Métro: Bastille

Le Fouquet's (C 2)

The classiest bar on the Champs-Elysées. Frequented by film and media crowd. Elegant international clientele. Pricey.
Daily until 02.00; 99, Avenue des Champs-Elysées (8th arr.); Métro: George V

Chez Georges (F 4)

⚘ Small bar in a lively St-Germain street. Always packed and pretty noisy. Good atmosphere. Cabaret and French *chanson* in the cellar.
Daily until 02.00; 11, Rue des Canettes (6th arr.); Métro: St-Germain-des-Prés

Harry's and Mabillou's New York Bar (E 2)

American bar popular with expats. Legend has it that this was where the Bloody Mary was invented. Expertly mixed cocktails and 160 different whiskies. A limited selection of snacks.
Daily until 04.00; 5, Rue Daunou (2nd arr.); Métro: Opéra

Hemingway Bar and L'Espadon in the Ritz (E 3)

Very elegant, but you don't have to be rich or famous to afford a drink in one of the exclusive hotel's two bars.
Daily until 03.00; 15, Place Vendôme (Entrance Rue Cambon, 1st arr.); Métro: Opéra

---

MARCO POLO SELECTION: ENTERTAINMENT

1 Les Bains
The best nightclub, but strict door policy (page 81)

2 Le Balajo
Traditional dance hall in the Bastille district (page 81)

3 La Chapelle des Lombards
Hot dance sounds and live music until dawn (page 81)

4 Le Bataclan
Major rock concert venue (page 81)

5 Théâtre National de Chaillot
Elegant modern theatre (page 86)

6 La Locomotive
Disco and live music in the Pigalle-Montmartre area (page 81)

7 New Morning
The best of the city's many jazz clubs (page 83)

8 Divan du Monde
Live music from around the world (page 82)

9 Le Queen
Wild and energetic club that's all the rage (page 81)

10 Grand Rex Cinema and Club
Europe's largest screen; club downstairs (pages 82 and 85)

L'Hôtel – Bar Le Bélier (F 4)

Romantic bar in the hotel where Oscar Wilde spent his last days.
Daily until 02.00; 13, Rue des Beaux-Arts (6th arr.); Métro: St-Germain-des-Prés

La Palette (F 4)

Near the *Ecole des Beaux Arts* this Left Bank bar is popular with students, locals and tourists alike. Big terrace.
Daily until 02.00, closed Sun; 43, Rue de Seine (6th arr.); Métro: St-Germain des Prés

Rosebud (E 6)

Legendary bar in Montparnasse, popular with film and media types. Atmospheric.
Daily until 02.00; 11, Rue Delambre (14th arr.); Métro: Vavin

DISCOS & NIGHTCLUBS

Whether you want an energetic night out on a pulsating dance floor, or a ballroom dancing session in an old-fashioned music hall, from Techno to Tango, Paris has it all. Most clubs don't get going until after midnight, and stay open until the early hours. Bear in mind that many of the trendier and so-called 'private' clubs can be selective about who they let in. Dressing up for the occasion may increase your chances of getting in.

Les Bains (G 3)

★ Converted Turkish bath where the smart set from the fashion and film worlds congregate. Renowned for its extremely selective door policy. Expensive.
7, Rue du Bourg-l'Abbé (3rd arr.); Tel. 01 48 87 01 80; Métro: Etienne Marcel

Le Balajo (I 4)

★ 🕺 Old-style dance hall once frequented by Edith Piaf, now one of the most popular hot spots in Paris. Monday is one of the best dance nights, with the focus on disco and the latest sounds.
9, Rue de Lappe (11th arr.); Tel. 01 47 00 07 87; Métro: Bastille

Le Banana Café (G 4)

Lively gay club in Les Halles.
Daily 17.00-05.00; 13, Rue de la Ferronnerie (1st arr.); Tel. 01 42 33 35 31; Métro: Châtelet

Le Bataclan (I 3)

★ Live music and theme nights.
50, Boulevard Voltaire (11th arr.); Tel. 01 44 75 52 65; Métro: Oberkampf

La Chapelle des Lombards (I 4)

★ 🕺 Samba, salsa, merengue and other Latin American sounds. Every night except Sundays.
19, Rue de Lappe (11th arr.); Tel. 01 43 57 24 24; Métro: Bastille

El Globo (G 2)

🕺 Huge disco with great music and a good crowd.
Sat only; 8, Boulevard de Strasbourg (10th arr.); Métro: Strasbourg St Denis

La Locomotive (F 1)

★ 🕺 Enormous three-storey disco with three dance floors to cater for different tastes. Very lively, mostly young crowd.
Daily (except Mon); 90, Boulevard de Clichy (18th arr.); Tel. 01 42 57 37 37; Métro: Blanche

Le Queen (C 2)

★ The hottest club in Paris. Essentially but not exclusively gay.
102, Avenue des Champs-Elysées (8th arr.); Tel. 01 42 89 31 41; Métro: George V

Rex-Club (G 2)

★ ᚦ Club in the basement of the Rex cinema. From heavy metal and rock to seventies soul, rap and reggae. Frequent live performances after midnight.

Daily, except Sun/Mon, from 23.00; 5, Boulevard Poissonnière (2nd arr.); Métro: Rue Montmartre

La Scala (F 3)

◉ ᚦ Huge venue spread across three floors. The décor is not all that up to date, but the music is. Very popular and always packed, with a predominantly teen crowd.

188, Rue de Rivoli (1st arr.); Tel. 01 42 61 64 00; Métro: Palais Royal

Le Shéhérazade (E 1)

ᚦ Wild dancing for the energetic.

Daily, except Sun/Mon, from 23.00; 3, Rue de Liège (8th arr.); Tel. 01 48 74 41 68; Métro: Liège

Le Tango (H 3)

African and Latin sounds predominate in this former tango palace. Relaxed atmosphere. Open for tango sessions on Saturday and Sunday afternoons. Karaoke once a week.

Closed Mon/Tues; 11, Rue au Maire (3rd arr.); Tel. 01 42 72 17 78; Métro: Arts et Métiers

There are plenty of places in Paris where you can go to listen to live music, and the choice can sometimes be overwhelming. Here are a few recommended venues, but for up-to-date listings and times check the daily newspapers or, better still, pick up one of the weekly listings magazines (see below) to see what's on.

Caveau de la Huchette (G 5)

Long-running jazz club in the heart of the Latin Quarter. New Orleans and trad jazz.

Daily from 22.00; 5, Rue de la Huchette (5th arr.); Tel. 01 43 26 65 05; Métro: St Michel

Le Divan du Monde (F 1)

★ On the weekends, this colourful jazz venue stages a variety of live music for a mixed crowd.

75, Rue des Martyres (18th arr.); Tel. 01 44 92 77 66; Métro: Pigalle

Le Duc des Lombards (G 4)

Different musicians every day. For jazz connoisseurs.

Daily until 04.00; 42, Rue des Lombards (1st arr.); Tel. 01 42 33 22 88; Métro: Châtelet Les Halles

---

What's On Where

There are a number of publications which provide detailed listings of plays, concerts, films, and other cultural and sporting events. For English speakers, *Pariscope* is probably the best as it includes a *Time Out* recommendations section and costs only 3 FF. *L'Officiel des Spectacles* is similar to *Pariscope* and costs only 2 FF, but doesn't have an English section. Both are issued on Wednesdays. *Nova* is a good monthly magazine with listings and ideas and costs 10 FF. You can also glean quite a lot of information from the daily papers. *Libération* and the Wednesday issue of *Le Figaro* are particularly good for listings. All are available at news-stands.

New Morning (G 2)

★ This converted factory may not look like a major venue from the outside, but all the big international jazz greats have played here – it's the centre of the jazz scene in Paris. The programme has diversified in more recent years to include other trends such as African, flamenco, salsa and Latin jazz. Get there early if you want a seat.

10, Rue des Petites-Ecuries (10th arr.); Tel. 01 45 23 51 41; Métro: Château d'Eau

Opus-Café (H 1)

ⵣ Unique venue by the Seine with pleasant atmosphere, live music, cocktails at the long bar, and restaurant.

Daily (except Sun) from 20.00; 167, Quai de Valmy (10th arr.); Tel. 01 40 38 09 57; Métro: Louis Blanc

Le Petit Opportun (G 4)

First-class jazz in a tiny venue. Always full.

15, Rue Lavandières-Ste-Opportune (1st arr.); Tel. 01 42 36 01 36; Métro: Châtelet

Le Slow Club (G 4)

Swing and Dixieland in the oldest jazz joint in town. An institution.

Daily (except Sat and Mon); 130, Rue de Rivoli (1st arr.); Tel. 01 42 33 84 30; Métro: Châtelet

Le Zénith (O)

ⵣ Part of the Parc de la Villette cultural complex, this stadium has a capacity to seat over 6000 people. It is the main venue in Paris for international rock and pop concerts.

26, Avenue Corentin Cariou (19th arr.); Tel. 01 42 40 27 28; Métro: Porte de Pantin, Porte de la Villette

CABARET

After more than 100 years, topless chorus girls in sequins and feathers are still doing the can-can in the Moulin Rouge. Nowadays, however, Parisian cabaret shows and music hall revues no longer resemble the raucous Bohemian scenes immortalized by Toulouse-Lautrec. The shows are slick, extravagant, and very kitsch, catering more or less exclusively for tourists and businessmen.

Crazy Horse Saloon (C 3)

Beautiful women in scanty clothes perform fairly uninspiring routines.

Shows: 21.00 and 23.00; Tickets from 300 FF; 12, Avenue George V (8th arr.); Tel. 01 47 23 32 32; Métro: Alma Marceau

Folies Bergère 2)

The dated revue has been revamped and given a new lease of life with a more contemporary programme.

32, Rue Richer (9th arr.); Tel. 01 44 79 98 98; Métro: Cadet, Rue Montmartre

Le Lapin Agile (F 1)

Oldest cabaret in Montmartre. Good atmosphere.

Daily (except Mon) 21.00-02.00; 22, Rue des Saules (18th arr.); Tel. 01 46 06 43 24; Métro: Lamarck Caulaincourt

Lido (C 2)

The best show of its type headed by the Bluebell Girls. The vast auditorium is always full.

Show: 22.00 and 24.00; from 500 FF; 116, Avenue des Champs-Elysées (8th arr.); Tel. 01 45 63 11 61; Métro: George V

Michou   (F 1)

Funny and entertaining transvestite cabaret near Pigalle.

Show: 21.00; Tickets from 200 FF; 80, Rue des Martyrs (9th arr.); Tel. 01 46 06 16 04; Métro: Pigalle

Moulin Rouge   (F 1)

Traditional showgirl revue in the birthplace of the cancan. Pigalle tourist trap.

Shows: 22.00 and 24.00; Tickets from 350 FF; 82, Boulevard de Clichy (9th arr.); Tel. 01 46 06 00 19; Métro: Blanche

Paradis Latin   (G 5)

Plenty of sumptuous costumes and a varied line-up.

Show: 22.00 (except Tues); Tickets from 350 FF; 28, Rue du Cardinal-Lemoine (5th arr.); Tel. 01 43 25 28 28; Métro: Cardinal Lemoine

CINEMAS

Paris, with its 300 cinema screens, is the perfect destination for film buffs. In the central cinemas, mainstream foreign films are generally shown in the original language with French subtitles, but sometimes they are dubbed into French. Check whether the film is in *v.o.* (*version originale*) or *v.f.* (*version française*). Most of the big screen cinema complexes showing the latest releases are concentrated in the Latin Quarter, in St-Germain-des-Prés, in Montparnasse, on the Champs-Elysées and around the Grands Boulevards. But there is an equally wide choice of art house and repertory cinemas. To find out what's on where consult the publications listed on page 82. Programmes change on Wednesdays.

La Géode: the gigantic spherical cinema in Parc de la Villette

La Cinémathèque Française

Regular screenings of classic and rare films, and interesting retrospectives for film buffs. Cheap.
(**B3**) *Palais de Chaillot, 9, Avenue Albert de Mun (16th arr.); Métro: Trocadéro*
(**C3**) *Palais de Tokyo, 13, Avenue du Président Wilson (16th arr.); Métro: Iéna, Alma Marceau*
(**G4**) *Centre Pompidou Salle Garance, Rue Rambuteau (3rd arr.); Métro: Hôtel de Ville*

La Géode (O)

♁ Giant spherical cinema screen showing science and nature films. Has to be seen to be believed. Part of the Parc de la Villette complex. Book in advance.
26, Avenue Corentin-Cariou (19th arr.); Tel. 01 40 05 06 07; Métro: Porte de la Villette

Grand Rex (G 2)

★ ♁ Gigantic cinema with 2800 seats and the biggest screen in Europe. But most films shown here tend to be dubbed into French.
1, Boulevard Poissonnière (2nd arr.); Tel. 01 42 36 83 93; Métro: Bonne Nouvelle

La Pagoda (D 5)

Prettiest cinema in Paris, set in a Japanese pagoda with gardens and tea house. Films shown here in their original language (v.o.) with French subtitles. 2 screens.
57, Rue de Babylon (7th arr.); Tel. 01 45 55 48 48; Métro: St François Xavier

Max Linder Panorama (G 2)

Huge screen and ultra-modern sound in an art deco theatre.
24, Boulevard Poissonnière (9th arr.); Tel. 01 48 24 88 88; Métro: Bonne Nouvelle

Videothèque de Paris (G 3)

Mecca for film buffs and filmmakers. Six or seven thematically linked films are screened in its three cinemas each day – the common theme is usually Paris.
Tues-Sat 12.30-21.00; 2, Grande Galerie-Porte St-Eustache (1st arr.); Tel. 01 40 26 34 30; Métro: Les Halles

CONCERTS

The Parisian music scene has vastly improved over the last few years. Annual international music festivals are organized by the Paris council, and a wide variety of classical and contemporary music concerts are performed in first-class venues throughout the year. In winter, concerts are held every afternoon in the Théâtre des Champs-Elysées, in the Salle Pleyel and in the Salle Gaveau. You can hear church recitals in the Madeleine, St-Germain-des-Prés, St-Roch, St-Séverin, Notre-Dame (the organ was restored in 1991) and in the Sainte-Chapelle. See pages 82 and 91 for details on ticket purchase.

Cité de la Musique (O)

A vast modern concert hall in the Parc de la Villette staging classical, contemporary, jazz, and world music performances.
221, Avenue Jean Jaurès (19th arr.); Tel. 01 44 84 44 84; Métro: Porte de Pantin

Salle Pleyel (C 1)

Most orchestral concerts are held here in the city's main concert hall, home to the *Orchestre de Paris*.
252, Rue du Faubourg St Honoré (8th arr.); Tel. 01 45 67 53 00; Métro: Ternes

OPERA & BALLET

Since the opening of the Opéra Bastille in 1989, the magnificent 19th-century Opéra de Paris Garnier is now used predominantly for ballet. The new ultra-modern national opera house has an exceptional, high-tech stage and a capacity to seat 2700 – the acoustics are so good that you can hear just as well from any seat in the auditorium.

Opéra de Paris Garnier (E 2)
Place de l'Opéra (11th arr.); Tel. 01 47 42 57 50; Métro: Opéra

Opéra de Paris Bastille (I 5)
Performances daily around 17.00 (except Tues/Sun); Entrance 20 FF; Tel. 01 40 01 19 70 or 01 43 57 42 14; Place de la Bastille (12th arr.); Métro: Bastille

THEATRE

With the exception of the summer months, when the focus shifts to the South of France, countless plays, including foreign productions, are staged in the 100 or so theatres and *café théâtres* across Paris. The high point of the drama season is the avant-garde Autumn Festival (see p. 77).

Athénée (E 2)
Lovely theatre near the Opéra that stages interesting productions.
4, Square de l'Opéra (9th arr.); Tel. 01 47 42 67 27; Métro: Opéra

Bouffes du Nord (H 1)
Amazing stage for Peter Brook's world-famous company.
37 bis, Boulevard de la Chapelle (10th arr.); Tel. 01 42 39 34 50; Métro: La Chapelle

La Cartoucherie (O)
Several avant-garde theatres, including the acclaimed *Théâtre du Soleil*, are housed in this former armaments factory in the Bois de Vincennes.
Route-du-Champ-de-Manoeuvres (12th arr.); Tel. 01 43 74 88 50; Métro: Château de Vincennes or No. 112 bus to Cartoucherie

Comédie Française (F 3)
France's national theatre was founded by Louis XIV in 1680. While it is principally a theatre for classical drama, it often includes modern productions in its seasonal programme. Cheap tickets for the upper circle are usually available from the box office on the night. Near the Louvre.
2, Rue de Richelieu (1st arr.); Tel. 01 40 15 00 15; Métro: Palais Royal

Lucernaire Forum (E 6)
Theatre and cinema complex with restaurant. Up to six performances per day.
53, Rue Notre-Dame-des-Champs (6th arr.); Tel. 01 45 44 57 34; Métro: Vavin

Odéon Théâtre de l'Europe (F 5)
Specializes in foreign plays performed in their original language.
Place de l'Odéon (6th arr.); Tel. 01 43 25 70 32; Métro: Odéon

Théâtre National de Chaillot (B 3)
★ Two lovely theatre spaces used to stage both mainstream and experimental productions.
Place du Trocadéro (16th arr.); Tel. 01 47 27 81 15; Métro: Trocadéro

Théâtre de la Ville (G4)
Chanson and dance.
Place du Châtelet (4th arr.); Tel. 01 42 74 22 77; Métro: Châtelet

Practical information

*Useful addresses, information and survival tips
alphabetically listed for quick reference*

BANKS & BUREAUX DE CHANGE

Normal banking hours are Mon-Fri 09.00-17.00 and a number of banks open on Sat until 12.00. Some of the smaller banks close for lunch from 12.30-14.30 and all day Monday. Bear in mind that not all banks have currency exchange facilities.

Visas and other common credit cards are widely accepted and can be used to withdraw cash from the bank or from a cash dispenser (don't forget your PIN number).

Bureaux de Change can be found all over the city, at the airports and in all the main stations. They stay open later than the banks, but their exchange rates are less favourable. In emergencies, there is also a 24-hour Automatic Money Changing Machine at *66 Champs-Elysées* (**C2**).

CUSTOMS

Although customs restrictions have now been lifted for goods imported between EU countries (provided they are for personal use), there are recommended restrictions: 90 litres wine, 10 litres spirits 800 cigarettes. For non-EU nationals the personal allowances are: 1 litre spirits or 2 litres fortified wine or 3 litres table wine; 200 cigarettes or 100 cigarillos or 50 cigars.

EMBASSIES

Australia: *4, Rue Jean-Rey (15th arr.);
Métro: Courcelles; Tel. 01 40 59 33 00*

Britain: *35, Rue du Faubourg St-Honoré (8th arr.); Métro: Concorde;
Tel. 01 44 51 31 00*

Canada: *35, Avenue Montaigne (8th arr.); Métro: Franklin D. Roosevelt;
Tel. 01 44 43 29 00*

Ireland (Eire): *4, Rue Rude (16th arr.); Métro: Charles de Gaulle-Etoile;
Tel. 01 44 17 67 00*

USA: *2, Avenue Gabriel (8th arr.);
Métro: Champs-Elysées-Clémenceau;
Tel. 01 43 12 22 22*

EMERGENCY NUMBERS

Ambulance/SAMU: 15
Fire: 18
Police: 17
Doctor: 01 47 07 77 77
Dentist: 01 43 37 51 00

INFORMATION

French Government Tourist Offices abroad

Britain: *178 Piccadilly, London W1V OAL; Tel. 0171 491 7622*

Ireland: *35, Lower Abbey Street, Dublin 1; Tel. 01 703 4046*

USA: *610 Fifth Ave. Suite 222, New York, NY 10020-2452; Tel. 212 757 1125*

Office du Tourisme et des Congrès de Paris

The central Paris tourist office on the Champs-Elysées offers an accommodation service for a small fee, brochures, city maps, museum guides, and information about city tours and excursions. *Daily 09.00-20.00; 127, Champs-Elysées; Tel. 01 49 52 53 54, Fax 01 49 52 53 00; Métro: Charles de Gaulle-Etoile* (**C2**)

Tourist offices can also be found in all the main stations and near the Eiffel Tower.

Gare du Nord: *Mon-Sat, May-Oct 08.00-21.00, Nov-Apr 08.00-20.00; in summer, Sun 13.00-20.00; Tel. 01 45 26 94 82* (**G1**)

Gare de l'Est: *Mon-Sat: May-Oct 08.00-21.00, Nov-Apr 08.00-20.00; Tel. 01 46 07 17 73* (**H1**)

Gare de Lyon: *Mon-Sat: May-Oct 08.00-21.00, Nov-Apr 08.00-20.00; Tel. 01 43 43 33 24* (**I6**)

Tour Eiffel: *Daily May-Sept 11.00-18.00; Tel. 01 45 51 22 15* (**B4**)

LOST PROPERTY

If you lose your passport or you are the victim of a theft, then you should fill out a *déclaration* in the nearest police station, especially if you wish to claim against your insurance. The chances of retrieving property you have lost in a public place are pretty slim, but it may be worth contacting the Lost Property Office: *Mon-Fri 09.00-17.00; 36, Rue des Morillons; Tel. 01 48 28 32 36; Métro: Convention* (**O**)

PARKING

Finding a free parking place on the streets of Paris is almost impossible. Make use of the efficient public transport system and avoid driving in the city centre if you can. If you do decide to drive, there are a number of underground car parks both on the outskirts of the city and in the centre. The daily tariff is around 100 FF. Bear in mind that car crime is a big problem in Paris, even in the supposedly secure car parks.

Parking Fines

Fines for illegal parking are very high in Paris. Rueful violators buy a stamp equivalent to the value of the fine at a *bureau de tabac* (tobacconist or bar bearing the *Tabac* sign) and send the parking ticket with the stamp attached to the appropriate police station. Many Parisians simply throw their parking tickets away or stuff them in the glove compartment. Then, come the next Presidential election, there's an amnesty on fines. But be warned: blatant violators of the parking restrictions risk having their vehicles towed away.

Abbesses Métro station: a fine example of Guimard's art nouveau design

PHARMACIES

24-hour chemist: *Pharmacie Dhéry 84, Avenue des Champs-Elysées (8th arr.); Tel. 01 45 62 02 41* (**C2**)

POST & TELEPHONE

Post offices (identified by the yellow *La Poste* sign) are open Mon-Fri 08.00-19.00 and Sat 08.00-12.00. The main post office is at *52, Rue du Louvre (1st arr.); Métro: Les Halles* (**F3**) and is open 24 hours. Stamps (*timbres*) can also be bought from tobaconnists (*tabac*).

You can make international calls from most public telephones, which also take incoming calls. Many kiosks accept coins (1, 2, 5 and 10 FF) but it is much easier and more economical to use a phonecard (*télécarte*). These come in units of 50 or 120 and can be bought from post offices, underground and mainline stations and tobacconists.

To phone abroad from France, dial 00, wait for the tone, then dial the country code (UK: 44, USA and Canada: 1, Ireland: 353, Australia: 61, New Zealand: 64), followed by the area code omitting the initial 0, and the subscriber number. The country code for France is 33. All telephone numbers in France are now 10 digits. You need to dial a 2 digit area code before the 8 digit subscriber number: 01 for Paris and the surrounding region, 02 for north-west France, 03 for the north-east, 04 for the south-east, and 05 for the south-west.

Using the bus, métro or RER trains is the fastest, cheapest and safest means of getting around. Nowhere in Paris is farther than 500 m from the nearest métro station. There are 13 métro lines, and a 14th is currently under construction. Each line is identified both by a number and the terminus stations at either end. The métro runs from 05.30 until 01.00, and the frequency of trains is every two to seven minutes.

The RER is a network of express rail lines that link the city centre with the suburbs. There are four lines (A, B, C and D) that run both under- and overground.

RER trains are particularly good for getting to and from the airport, or for destinations outside the city such as Versailles or Euro Disney. Route maps for the RER and métro can be obtained from most stations and tourist offices. You will also find one inside the back cover of this guide.

Every station has ticket booths and some have coin-operated machines. Each ticket is valid for one journey on the métro, bus or RER (zones 1 and 2 only). It is cheaper to buy métro tickets in batches of ten – ask for a *carnet* (46 FF). Children under 10 pay half price and children under four travel free. You must validate your ticket at the entrance and exit barriers.

WEATHER IN PARIS

Seasonal averages

Daytime temperatures in °C

Jan	Feb	Mar	Apr	May	June	July	Aug	Sep	Oct	Nov	Dec
6	7	12	16	20	23	25	24	21	16	10	7

Night-time temperatures in °C

Jan	Feb	Mar	Apr	May	June	July	Aug	Sep	Oct	Nov	Dec
1	1	4	6	10	13	15	14	12	8	5	2

Sunshine: hours per day

Jan	Feb	Mar	Apr	May	June	July	Aug	Sep	Oct	Nov	Dec
2	3	5	7	7	7	7	7	6	4	4	4

Rainfall: days per month

Jan	Feb	Mar	Apr	May	June	July	Aug	Sep	Oct	Nov	Dec
12	10	8	9	9	9	9	9	9	8	10	10

Travel passes are practical and good value, and are also valid for the whole transport network. The one-day *Formule 1* pass costs 30 FF for central Paris and 40 FF for Paris and the suburbs. The *Paris Visite* card costs 80 FF for two days and 110 FF for three days, and also gives discounts in some museums. The weekly Carte Orange Paris pass is valid from Monday to Sunday and costs 72 FF. The monthly *Carte Orange Paris* costs 243 FF but you can only buy it at the start of the month. You need a passport-size photo for the *Carte Orange* passes, which can be bought in any métro station. *Formule 1* and *Paris Visite* cards need no photo, and can be bought in most métro stations and tourist offices, at the RATP (Paris transport company) office, *53, Quai des Grands-Augustins*, and the kiosk by the *Place de la Madeleine* flower market.

Buses run between 07.00 and 20.30 (some routes until 00.30) on weekdays, with a reduced service on Sundays. Route maps are displayed inside and outside buses and at bus stops. If you do not have a métro ticket, you can buy a ticket from the driver. Bear in mind that longer bus journeys require more than one ticket. All tickets must be cancelled in the machine on the bus. There are 10 night buses which run between 01.00 and 05.00 from Châtelet.

TAXIS

Taxi fares are relatively cheap, but cost a bit more at night, on Sundays and public holidays, and in the suburbs. Supplements are charged for journeys to and from airports and stations, for luggage weighing more than 5 kg, and for a fourth passenger or an animal. These extras are regulated, and should be clearly shown on the meter. Taxis can be hailed on the street, except in the vicinity of a taxi rank or a railway station. The taxi sign on the roof of the vehicle is illuminated when the taxi is free.

To make a complaint contact: *Service des Taxis-Préfecture de Police, 36, Rue des Morillons (15th arr.); Tel. 01 45 31 14 80; Métro: Convention.* If you lose or leave an article in a taxi: *Tel. 01 45 31 14 80, ext. 42 08.*

Private taxi companies:

G 7 Radio: Tel. 01 47 39 47 39
Alpha-taxis: Tel. 01 45 85 85 85
Artaxi: Tel. 01 42 41 50 50 and 01 43 35 00 00; Advance booking from 1 hour to 8 days: Tel. 01 42 08 64 59
Taxi-Bleus: Tel. 01 49 36 10 10
Taxi Radio Etoile: Tel. 01 42 70 41 41
Airport Shuttle; Tel. 01 45 38 55 72; Advance booking; 120 FF, cheaper for groups of more than 2 people

THEATRE TICKETS

The main *Office du Tourisme* sells tickets for the revue theatres. Other ticket agencies include:

Alpha – FNAC   (G 3)

Concert and theatre tickets.
Forum des Halles; 1, Rue Pierre Lescot (1st arr.); Tel. 01 40 41 40 00; Métro: Châtelet Les Halles

Le Kiosque Théâtre

Theatre tickets for the same evening at half price.
15, Place de la Madeleine (8th arr.); Daily (except Mon) 12.30-20.00; Métro: Madeleine (E2) or Châtelet Les Halles RER station, at the meeting point (G3); Daily (except Sun, Mon and public holidays) 12.30-20.00

S.O.S. Théâtres   (C 2)
20 % commission charge.
Mon-Fri 10.00-19.00, Sat 10.00-17.00; 73, Avenue des Champs-Elysées (8th arr.); Tel. 01 42 25 67 07; Métro: George V

TIPPING

15% service is always included on the bill in a restaurant or café. It is customary, however, to leave a tip of up to 10% after a meal and a couple of extra francs for the waiter in a café – but this is by no means obligatory. The normal rate for taxis is also about 10%. Usherettes in cinemas and theatres get no less than 2 FF, and cloakroom attendants not less than 5 FF. Hairdressers would expect about 10 FF. In hotels, it is also customary to tip the chambermaid, and room service should not be forgotten either.

TOURS

Bus tours
Balabus: This tour bus runs between Gare de Lyon and La Défense, passing many sites along the way. You can jump on and off as you please. A one-day ticket costs the same as three métro tickets. Even the locals use Balabus to see Paris on a Sunday.
April-Sept, Sun afternoon and public holidays only

Bus Paris Vision and Cityrama: 2-hour city tours, 150 FF per person

Paribus – Les Cars Rouges: a tour of all the sights on a double-decker bus. You can get off wherever you like and continue your tour on any of the following buses. Commentaries are given in English.

Daily from 10.00-20.00, departures every 50 minutes; 2-day pass 125 FF for adults, 60 FF for children; Tel. 01 42 30 55 50 and 01 45 30 55 76

Batobus
River tours. There are five stops: Eiffel Tower, Musée d'Orsay, Musée du Louvre, Notre-Dame and Hôtel de Ville. You can choose a single tour or buy a day pass which allows you to embark and disembark wherever and as often as you want.
Daily (May-Sept) from 10.00-20.00, departures every 45 mins; One journey 12 FF, day ticket 65 FF

Canal Tours
A great way to see the old canals and city waterways (see page 25).
Canauxrama: Tel. 01 42 39 15 00
Paris Canal: Tel. 01 42 40 96 97

Chauffeur Service
London Cab Paris: Tel. 01 43 70 18 18

Cycle Tours
Cycling round Paris can be a fairly hair-raising experience and is not really advisable. This is not a city built for cyclists. There are very few cycle paths and motorists are unaccommodating. If you feel like a cycle, however, then go along to the Bois de Vincennes where you can hire a bike and ride around the park at your leisure. For organized cycle tours around town contact *Paris-Vélo*: *Tel. 01 43 37 59 22.*

Walking Tours
One of the best ways to see Paris is on foot. There are many guided walks around Paris organized for locals and tourists alike. You can find details in any of the main listings guides (see page 82).

Do's and don'ts

Some of the dangers and tourist traps to watch out for

Aperitifs and wine

Some of the bars and cafés around the main tourist areas may try to persuade you to have one of their 'special' aperitifs. As a rule, these are expensive and rarely that special. If you are offered a Kir (blackcurrant liqueur with white wine) or a Kir Royale (with champagne), bear in mind that the quality of the wine is not always guaranteed. In restaurants, however, ordering the house wine (*le vin du patron*) is generally a safe bet.

Bad food

The pedestrian zones around Rue de la Huchette in the lower section of the Boulevard St-Michel and the Rue Mouffetard in the Latin Quarter are notorious for their bad quality restaurants. An exception to this general rule are the North African restaurants dotted around these areas, whose couscous-based menus are usually very good.

Boat trips

When the water level in the river is low, a boat trip can be a frustrating experience because it then becomes difficult to see above the quay walls that border the Seine.

The running commentaries on the *bateaux-mouches* are not always that enlightening and sometimes difficult to understand. Some companies offer lunch and dinner cruises, but the quality of the food is often disappointing.

Limousines

The chauffeur driven limousines that you see parked outside airports and railway stations, identified by the *Voiture de Place* sign, are often mistaken for taxis. You may be tempted to hop into one if the taxi queue is long, but be warned, such a luxury comes at a price.

Louvre marathon

A visit to the Louvre is a must, if only to see the Pyramid and a few of the masterpieces. But to attempt to cover the whole museum in one visit will only leave you feeling frustrated and exhausted. The Louvre is so vast that it would take a lifetime to see all its treasures properly. Entrance fees are half-price on Sundays and it gets very crowded, especially in the afternoons. It is usually much quieter on Mondays and Wednesdays when the museum stays open until 21.45.

Perfume

Given that Paris is regarded as one of the world centres of the perfume industry, it may come as a surprise that perfume costs more here than in any other European city. If you do want to bring some back, stick to the duty-free shops or try one of the discount stores.

Place du Tertre

Once a romantic and atmospheric spot, the Place du Tertre is now one of the worst tourist traps in Paris. Each year more than a million tourists squeeze themselves into this tiny square, most of them coach parties. They are enticed into the restaurants, bars, cafés and cabarets which abound in and around the area. As a rule the prices these establishments charge are high and the quality poor. Around 250 street artists have been given an official permit to be here, but there are just as many operating here illegally. Some of them can be quite pushy and intimidating. If you are persuaded to have your portrait done, make sure you establish a price beforehand – they can cost anything from 50 to 200 FF.

If you want to see the Sacré-Coeur, you can avoid the thronging Place du Tertre by climbing up through the narrow backstreets, which are quieter and still very picturesque. With such a big landmark to guide you, it is very difficult to get lost.

Red-light districts

Pigalle still thrives on its reputation as the sex and sleaze centre of Paris, attracting coachloads of tourists who peer into the sex shops and are bullied into strip joints where they are quickly relieved of much of their cash. The Rue St-Denis is the other well-known red-light district, where male and female prostitutes ply their trade. Both areas, however, are gradually being cleaned up as seedy bars and cabaret venues are being turned into trendy cafés and nightclubs. The Rue Ste-Anne in the Opéra district is where gay, transvestite and under-age prostitutes gather. While these areas are not overtly dangerous, it is prudent to avoid wandering through the backstreets late at night. The Bois de Boulogne should definitely be avoided after dark.

Theft

When compared to other major capital cities, there is relatively little violent crime in Paris. Petty theft, however, is all too common. Watch out for pickpockets on the métro and in crowded tourist areas, and only carry as much cash with you as you need.

Busking in the Métro

Tramps or *clochards* have always been part of Parisian life and are treated with a sort of resigned tolerance. But in the last few years the number of beggars has increased dramatically and there are more and more young people begging on the métro. Even if you want to help out with a few coins, you have to be selective – not all of these 'music makers' play a friendly tune.

INDEX

This index lists the main places, sights and hotels mentioned in this guide.
Illustrations are shown in italics. Main entries are in bold.

What do you get for your money?

 French bank notes come in denominations of 20, 50, 100, 200 and 500 FF and there are coins of 1, 2, 5, 10 and 20 FF, and 5, 10, 20 and 50 centimes. Here are a few prices to give you an idea of what your money is worth: a trip to the top of the Eiffel Tower in the lift costs 57 FF, whereas it costs only 14 FF to reach the second stage on foot; a bus tour of the city costs around 150 FF; postcards are between 2 and 6 FF and require a 3 FF stamp (within Europe); a small beer (un démi), ie 0.25 l, costs between 10 and 20 FF (cheaper at the bar than on a terrace); theatre tickets range from 60 to 250 FF; cinema tickets are around 50 FF (less on Mondays); a 3-minute international call to any European country (peak rate) is around 5 FF; an average taxi journey across the city centre costs around 60 FF (excess baggage is 5 FF extra per item); a croissant costs between 5 and 10 FF; the price of a small black coffee (express) varies from 5 FF to 25 FF depending on where you are drinking it.

 Most hotels, shops and restaurants accept credit cards. For further information on banks and currency exchange see page 87.

£	FF	FF	£
1	9.70	5	0.52
2	19.40	10	1.03
3	29.10	15	1.55
4	38.80	20	2.06
5	48.50	25	2.58
6	58.20	30	3.09
7	67.90	35	3.61
8	77.60	40	4.12
9	87.30	50	5.15
10	97.00	75	7.73
15	145.50	100	10.31
20	194.00	150	15.46
25	242.50	200	20.62
30	291.00	250	25.77
40	388.00	300	30.93
50	485.00	500	51.55
75	727.50	750	77.32
100	970.00	1000	103.09
250	2425.00	5000	515.46
500	4850.00	7500	773.20
1000	9700.00	10000	1030.93

The conversion table above is based on the Thomas Cook sell rate, February 98